Surviving Strong

(A Saxon Saga)

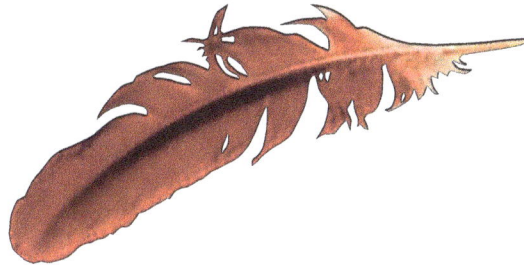

By Susan D. Brandenburg

Front Cover Photo:
    Jeannette (Jean) Saxon Acree - Picture Day - 1st Grade

It was a day caught in time by the brave photograph of a thin little girl with a smudged face wearing an over-sized red coat and smiling shyly, despite the insensitive cruelty of her teacher. "Wait a minute," the teacher had loudly told the photographer as she spit on a tissue and swiped at the grime on Jean's cheeks, pushing her hair back with a bobby pin and grabbing a large red coat from the closet. "This girl's dress is too dirty for a picture. I'll put a coat on her."

Surviving Strong

(A Saxon Saga)

By Susan D. Brandenburg

ISBN: 978-0-9915574-2-4

This book was published in the U.S.A. by Susan the Scribe, Inc.
www.susanthescribe.com

Illustrations by Patricia Setser

Book and Cover Design by Andie Jackson
Wonderdog Designs, Jacksonville, Florida

Dedicated to Emmett R. Saxon, Jr. Harry E. Acree and Bruce W. Acree ...

Gone, but never forgotten ...

Each man was integral to the success of the Saxon family.

Table of Contents

This book chronicles the dramatic, true story of the five Saxon siblings and their determined efforts to grow into productive, caring citizens, able to compete with the best of them despite their rough start in life. It is also the story of children born into abject poverty, torn apart by circumstances beyond their control, and joyfully reunited many decades later.

The purpose of this book is not to point a finger at anyone living or dead who was involved with the lives of these five children, but to encourage and inspire others who face similar challenges. At a time of global turmoil for our nation, as the battles of World War II and the Korean War ensued, a young woman married a man twice her age and gave birth to five children. Having lost her mother at a young age and been responsible for helping to raise her brothers and sisters, Christine Saxon was uneducated and had never known the love of a mother when she was deserted by her alcoholic husband and left to raise her children on her own. Society considered the Saxon siblings "throw-away kids," and expected nothing of them.

Jeannette, the oldest, was terrified of being left alone, but stayed with the younger children many nights when her parents were not at home. The oldest boy, Emmett, looked at the world through hungry eyes dulled by too much abuse and neglect. The youngest boy, Ben, was angry, often defiant, and desperate for attention. Clyde Dean, the baby, wailed ravenously, thirsty for food, milk and motherly love. Paula, whose birth certificate simply read "Baby Saxon," never knew her birth mother at all.

If you are at a place in your life where you can identify with any or all of the challenges faced by the Saxon siblings, it is their hope you will be inspired by their own true story; that you will gain insight and understanding about the abilities within you for compassion, tenacity and problem solving; that you will look in the mirror and recognize your own innate ability to overcome adversity through sheer determination. Tomorrow is a new day. Take the lessons learned from yesterday, accept them and build on them as you move forward and achieve your goals.

This is the Saxon Saga ... it may disturb some ... but it should serve as a springboard of encouragement for others to overcome adversity and achieve a successful life journey.

Cast of Characters

William H. Fleming "Pop"
      Father of Christine Fleming Saxon
            Grandfather of Jeannette, Emmett Jr., Ben, and Clyde Dean

Emmett Richmond Saxon Sr. and Christine Fleming Saxon –
      Parents of Jeannette, Emmett, Ben and Clyde Dean

Jeannette (Jean) Saxon Acree
      Daughter of Emmett Sr. & Christine Saxon
            Wife of Harry Acree
                  Mother of Bruce, Dianna (Sissy) and Stacy Acree

Emmett Richmond Saxon, Jr.
      Son of Emmett Sr. and Christine Saxon
            Husband of Helen Hendrix
                Father of Loressa Jeannette Saxon

Ben Lee Saxon
      Son of Emmett Sr. and Christine Saxon
            Former Husband of Kathy Elaine Perkins
            Father of Meredith and Robert Saxon

Clyde Dean (Emmaline – Emily) Saxon Scoggins Mullings
      Daughter of Emmett Sr. and Christine Saxon
            (Adopted by Virgil & Cecile Scoggins)
               Wife of Roger Mullings
                 Mother of Glenn, Michael and Scott Mullings

Paula Woodall Manning
      Daughter of Christine Saxon
            (Adopted by Frances and Paul Woodall)
               Former wife of Donald Rex Ledbetter, Sr./Larry Manning
               Mother of Donald, Dennis, Pollyanna & Petrina Ledbetter

fire!

Steps dragging, thin shoulders bowed in defeat, the young mother trudged down the hot, sandy Alabama dirt road. Carrying her youngest, Clyde Dean, in her arms, Christine Saxon was followed by Jeannette (Jean) and Emmett Jr. (ages seven and five), and, trailing far behind them, two-year old Ben. Nobody paid any attention to the little boy running behind, bawling at the top of his lungs and bounding along on the burning clay surface, his bare feet blistered and the hot sun beating down on his flaxen head. Clinching his fists and stomping his feet, Ben Saxon howled even louder. They all knew why he was so mad, and nobody even looked back. Mother was carrying the baby; she was not carrying Ben. That baby girl had replaced him in his mother's arms and it wasn't fair. It just wasn't fair! Wiping his grimy, tear-stained face with the back of his hand, he ran to catch up with the others. Ben was hot and thirsty, but most of all, he was mad!

They were homeless and Ben knew it was partly his fault. He and his big brother Emmett had been playing with wood and paper by the fireplace and Pop's log cabin had caught fire and burned to the ground. Well, they didn't mean to do it. It wasn't their fault nobody paid any attention to them! Pop (their grandfather) had been sitting right there in his rocking chair reading the newspaper as usual, Uncle Hoyt was outside and Mother had been cooking home-brew in the kitchen, as usual. Jean had been watching that baby, as usual. Then sparks were flying, the baby was screaming, flames were shooting up the wall and everybody was running for their lives! Now, here they were, walking down this dirt road toward Aunt Bebe's place, hoping she'd give them food and shelter.

Life wasn't fair! Ben kicked at the dirt with his bare feet. Yesterday they'd at least had a floor to sleep on and a roof over their heads, but now that shack was a smoldering pile of ashes. Ben felt like his feet were going to burst into flames, too. He was hot! He was sad! He was thirsty! He was mad!

It was 1948. Times were hard. Christine's husband, Emmett Richmond Saxon Sr., the father of her four children, had left them high and dry. An alcoholic and the "black sheep" of his prominent Tallahassee family, Emmett had met Christine Fleming in the orange groves of Lake Alfred, Florida and they had married in Deerfield Beach, Florida in 1940. The Saxons had barely eked out a living ever since.

Emmett Richmond Saxon Sr. was born into an illustrious family with bloodlines going back to the American pioneers, many of them pillars in their communities.

Emmett had the opportunities and physical attributes to achieve success. He might have been a good man but for his weakness for alcohol. Sadly, by the time his children came along, Emmett cared for little except where he would get his next drink.

The Saxon family frequently found shelter in abandoned gas stations and line shacks near the orange groves where Emmett drove a flatbed produce truck for the pickers and cut wood for his home brew. Producing baby after baby and hitting the beer joints at night, Emmett and Christine drifted aimlessly from one day to the next, with no plans beyond where they would lay their heads to sleep and where they would find the next drink. They gave little thought and even less attention to their children, treating them as minor inconveniences that required intermittent care and feeding.

When her husband deserted the family shortly after Emily's birth, Christine approached his well-to-do Tallahassee family, begging for help, but was flatly refused. Uneducated and unprepared to support a family, she'd found work as a barmaid, leaving six-year old Jeannette to watch the younger children. Finally, Christine's father, William H. Fleming, sent for his daughter and her kids to come live with him and his older son, Hoyt, in Oneonta, Alabama.

While young Ben's anguish echoed loudly up and down the back-country road, his siblings suffered in silence. Jeannette (called Jean) was almost seven years old, and desperately afraid of being left behind. Born July 23, 1941, and the oldest of the four, Jean walked carefully in her mother's shadow, remembering the terrifying times when her parents had left her to watch the little ones and stayed away all night long. Each time, Jean was afraid they would never come back. Now, her daddy really had left them for good. Poor mother … she had taken them to Pop's place in Alabama and the boys had burned it down. What was going to happen next? Jean hated the uncertainty of it all as her bare feet slapped on the dirt road and her throat ached for a drink of cool water. Beneath the filthy, soot-covered, too-short dress, Jean's little heart beat so hard it felt like it was going to burst out of her chest. What if mother went off and left them, too? Jean didn't know what was next, but she was staying as close to her mother as she could. She was not going to get left behind … no way!

Pop and Bruce

Nicknamed "Pop" by the children, Christine's father was one of the few constants in their lives. A man of strength, tall, sinewy, and pencil-thin, "Pop" always walked from place to place, wore a hat, smoked cigars, read newspapers and any books he could get his hands on, drank a raw egg with his grits every morning, and had a deep, abiding affection for these four little urchins his daughter, Christine, had birthed. They had been living in his log cabin until the day the boys burned it down.

Five year old Emmett Jr. walked aimlessly behind his big sister, his eyes to the ground and his thoughts scattered. Born August 4, 1943, Emmett Jr. had seen too much sadness in his short time on earth. He'd slept on too many hard floors in too many hovels, felt the hole of hunger in his belly too many times. He had too often watched helplessly as his mother was beaten by his drunken daddy, or worse, as daddy turned his angry eyes toward Emmett Jr. He was beyond the loud anger expressed by his little brother. Emmett Saxon, Jr. was numb. Life had beaten the anger right out of him. He had ceased to care about much of anything except the next meal.

Unlike his brother, Ben cared about everything, and he let it be known. From the very beginning, Ben was different. A skinny tow-headed little boy, third in the "stair-step lineup," he was the only one of the four Saxon kids to be born in a hospital (on December 5th, 1945 in Winter Haven, Florida). Maybe that healthy start gave him an extra boost of determination, or maybe he inherited these traits from strong pioneer ancestors, but whatever brought it on, Ben's determination to rise above his circumstances was innate and his bitter anger fueled that determination. The earliest example of that steel resolve was when his mother was about to give birth to Clyde Dean (Emily) and she asked her husband to get the kids out of the house. Two year old Ben balked, refusing to leave his mother's side. He didn't want to go anywhere with that man who was called his dad and he was worried about his mother. He put up such a fuss that his mother told them to leave without him. Although he remembers little of the actual birth of his baby sister, Ben was sitting on the bed when Clyde Dean (named after her father's sister, Clyde) was born on August 26, 1947.

Young Ben now had to share the same baby bed with his little sister and he didn't like it one bit. He remembers pulling the nipple out of the baby bottle. He remembers standing at the screen door crying while the baby in the little bed joined in the chorus, both of them desperately hungry and begging to be fed.

Clyde Dean was just over a year old when the boys burned Pop's house down. Before Jean could scoop her up and run down the steps to escape, a burning ember stuck to the back of the baby's neck, leaving a permanent scar. She would not know the origin of that scar until well into her adulthood. Clyde Dean (now Emily) was separated from her siblings within a year of that fire in 1948 and didn't see them again until 1985 when her still determined brother, Ben, tracked her down and brought her back into the family. It was then that the Saxon saga continued for Emily, as it does to this day.

For a while, after the house fire, Christine and her kids drifted from relative to relative within her family, the unkempt children washing themselves and their clothing when they could, sleeping on floors and porches, eating lumpy grits and leftovers – whatever anyone could spare – and spending much of their time alone as their mother found work at bars and juke joints along the way. Finally, Pop came through once again, sending for them to move into an apartment with him above a beer joint in Birmingham, Alabama, where Christine got a job.

By then, Jean was seven years old and forced to repeat first grade because she had missed so much school the year before, but the little girl's fear of being left behind was so strong that they couldn't keep her at the new school. When her mother or grandfather delivered her to the classroom, she would somehow escape and beat them back to the apartment nearly every time. One of Christine's sisters, Betty, also lived in the apartment and she complained loudly about being stuck cooking grits for the kids day and night while their mother went out on dates. As always, food was scarce and grits were their staple for breakfast, lunch and dinner. Emmett Jr. would later suffer from Rickets because of their erratic and unhealthy eating habits.

Undisciplined, unschooled, unsupervised and unruly, the Saxon kids ran wild in that apartment above the beer joint. One day, Jean was walking down the stairs when an old man looked at her. She took off running, but not before Pop saw what had happened and made a hard decision. No one was really watching these kids, he realized, and they were living in a dangerous place. He had to get them to safety and the only way he knew how to do that was to call Child Welfare and get some help. After investigating the unsavory situation, Child Welfare recommended that the children (all but Clyde Dean, who was too young) be placed in the Mercy Home, an orphanage in Woodlawn, Alabama, and that's where Pop sent them.

At just under three years old, Ben was the youngest child ever accepted at the Mercy Home. He was separated from his older brother and sister immediately, despite the fact that all of them were screaming for one another and fighting the separation with everything they had in them.

The baby, Clyde Dean (now Emily), was placed in one foster home, and then another, and eventually adopted by a loving family. She was the lucky one. Searching her mind for the earliest memories, Emily vaguely remembers her mother calling her "Ricky." Her next memory is sitting in the back seat of a car at about 2 ½ years old being driven by a social worker on the way to the foster home. "I remember another young girl was in the car with me and we were both crying. The social worker gave us both tiny little sewing machines that actually had moving parts. It made me feel better." Her foster home memories are pleasant, with one white haired lady called "Granny" who gave her a doll and put her to sleep in a tall feather bed, fed her salmon patties and played games with her. In a second foster home, Emily was in a crib taking a nap when she swallowed a penny. She told the man in charge and he assured her she would be okay, that "it would all come out in the end."

When she was 5½ years old, on May 7th, 1953, Clyde Dean was legally adopted by Virgil and Cecile Scoggins of Anniston, Alabama, and given the name Emmaline, after a great grandma. She grew up as Emmaline Scoggins, aware that she had been adopted, always quietly curious about her birth family but knowing she was loved by her adopted parents. "My adopted family had a beautiful home and I had my own room with brand new furniture," she recalls. "I rarely slept in my room as it was too far from anybody and I would get scared and have "nightmares." Nightmares, indeed … the little girl had a burn scar on her neck and a burning desire, like her older sister, not to be left alone. Looking back, Emmaline (now Emily) marvels at how deeply her adoptive parents loved her and how blessed she was to have them. "I'm sure I put a crimp in their love life," she says, smiling. "They bought me a twin bed and put it right next to their big bed in their room and I slept there holding Mama's hand all night long for many years – at least until I was about ten, when we moved to Vicksburg."

Emmaline's
Loving Adoptive Parents,
Virgil and Cecile Scoggins

It would be nearly four decades before Emily was reunited with the family she didn't remember; nearly four decades before she would be once again enfolded in the arms of the sister who scooped her up, brushed the burning ember from her neck, and saved her life.

For eight-year old Jean Saxon, the nightmares of being left behind were reality. Her worst fears had been realized and she had nowhere to turn at the Mercy Home. Jean had been left behind by her family and they were not coming back to get her. Not only had she lost the little sister she had carried on her hip almost from birth, but she was suddenly separated from the two brothers she had been charged to watch. Jean, a quiet loner by nature, suddenly found herself in a dorm with a bunch of other girls who were complete strangers.

Emmett, age six, was also separated from his siblings and placed with strangers in an unfamiliar setting. His only defense against the harsh reality of his life was a practiced nonchalance. Emmett Jr. simply acted as if he didn't care what happened to him.

At just three years of age, Ben was bitterly and loudly angry. Separated by age and gender, Ben begged constantly for his big sister and brother, all to no avail. "They tried every way they could to beat the defiance out of me, both verbally and physically, but nothing worked," Ben recalls. "I was still just as hard-headed and determined as ever."

The Saxon siblings had never been separated. Now, they were each on their own, but resolved to be reunited again. That resolve was ingrained, and nearly as strong as the survival instincts they had learned by necessity. Ultimately, those survival instincts combined with hard work, determination and a deep compassion for their fellow human beings would translate into success in later life for each of them.

The Mercy Home was run by the ladies of the Red Feather Society* (which has since evolved into United Way of Central Alabama). The name Red Feather (a Lakota symbol for strong warrior) has ironic correlations to the warrior heart of Ben Saxon, a veteran of many battles for respect, self-worth and identity, as well as to pride in the American Indian blood that is part of the Saxon heritage.

Although they professed to be Christian ladies, there to provide compassion-ate care for orphans and children who were victims of poverty and homelessness, the women who ran the Mercy Home had strange ways of showing mercy. With girls and boys housed in separate areas and divided by age, they showed no mercy to Jean despite the fact that she repeatedly begged to see her brothers. There were no visits allowed for the siblings. Jean, who had endured hunger, poverty, and neglect, had now lost her only anchors. She was alone as she had never been alone in her life.

Even before Emmett, Ben and Emily came along, Jean was part of a family, albeit the least important part. Her father would take her to the beer joint and sit her on a bar stool next to him while he was drinking. She'd sit quietly beside him for hours, without even a glass of water to quench her thirst or a cracker to stem her hunger. Sometimes, daddy took her to the grocery store where he bought sugar, yeast and other ingredients for that smelly home brew her mother cooked on the wood-burning stove.

"Jean, make sure he brings me a coconut cake," her mother would holler as she left with her dad for the grocery store. She'd make sure he remembered because if he did, she might even get a piece of that delicious cake. Jean was always hungry. After her brothers came along, all three of them would cry for food and their mother would tell them to go put bacon grease and sugar on a biscuit, if she had any. Jean remembers her mother's biscuits to this day – light and fluffy and delicious, even when they were the only morsel of food she had. The Saxons generally lived near a lake or on the edge of a swamp, where Christine could catch fish for dinner or shoot a duck, but whatever she had on hand to cook had to be kept warm until daddy got home. No one ate until he ate.

There were no bathroom facilities in the places where the Saxon family lived in Florida – only outhouses – and there was rarely an inside source of water. They washed what clothes they had and bathed, when weather permitted, in the nearby lakes or in an outside washtub. When it was cold, neither bodies nor clothing were washed.

The weather was chilly and no washing had been done when picture day at school rolled around during Jean's short time in first grade in Haines City, Florida.

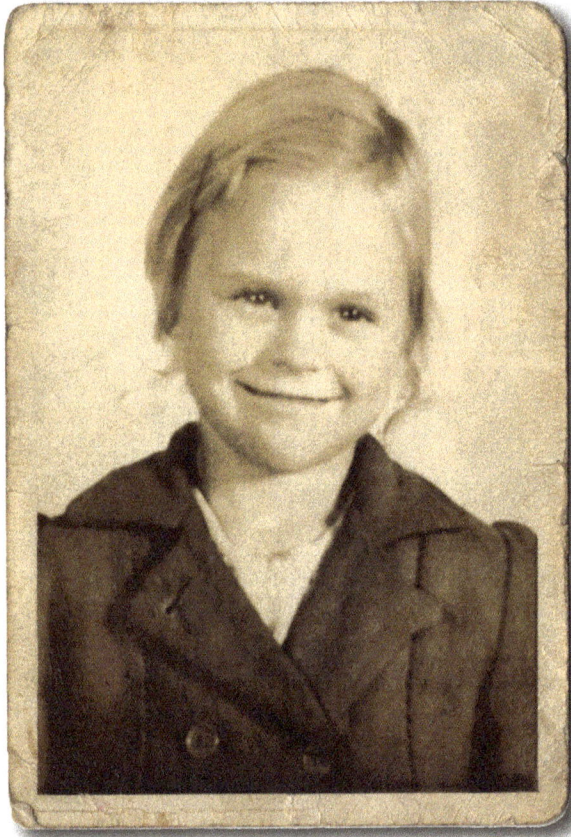

Jean Saxon
Picture Day, First Grade

It was a day caught in time by the brave photograph of a thin little girl with a smudged face wearing a red coat and smiling shyly, despite the insensitive cruelty of her teacher. "Wait a minute," the teacher had loudly told the photographer as she spit on a tissue and swiped at the grime on Jean's cheeks, pushing her hair back with a bobby pin and grabbing a large red coat from the closet. "This girl's dress is too dirty for a picture. I'll put a coat on her."

Jean never forgot that day. Even now, more than six decades later, her eyes become misty when she thinks of that innocent little girl who eagerly came to school to learn how to read and write and do arithmetic and, instead, learned firsthand about the ruthlessness that can reside behind the false smile on a teacher's face. Many years later, when Jean had the opportunity to stand in front of a classroom, she remembered that moment well and practiced such extraordinary kindness and concern that she received awards and accolades for her unstinting service to her students. Jean's brother, Ben, never forgot her picture day either, and as a result of that and many other hard lessons learned over the years, he has devoted his life to being the teacher that children want and need.

Soon after picture day, the Saxon family moved again. "Get the broom and get them boys out of here!" Jean's mother would say to her just before they cleared out and moved to another shack in another orange grove.

But now, here she was at the Mercy Home, separated from her brothers, her mother and her grandfather – no broom, no boys, no family at all.

Jean didn't cry. She just squared her shoulders and did what it took to stay out of trouble and survive. "None of us cried much at the Mercy Home, as I recall," she says today, remembering that although neither she nor her brothers ever felt anything but love for their grandfather, he was destined to spend the rest of his life feeling guilty for placing them at the Mercy Home. On the day of his funeral, "Pop" appeared in a vision at the foot of Jean's bed and woke her from a sound sleep, saying, 'I just want to thank you for coming to my funeral and forgiving me for what I did to you and the boys." Jean reached her hand out to touch him, but he was gone.

"I wanted to tell him there was nothing to forgive. There's no telling what would have happened to us if we hadn't gone to the Mercy Home."

* Red Feather Society

The Lakota Red Feather Society has been a part of the Warrior Society since the beginning of time. The Warrior Society comes in three societies: *Toka La Society* - modern day society - tribal police officer, *Strong Heart Society* - modern day society - helping veteran society, and *Akicita Society* - modern day society - soldier in making of a warrior, fighting. From this, the Lakota Warrior will always be protecting land/county and people. A warrior must go out of his way to protect, fight and beyond. If a warrior happens to be three times wounded, a special ceremony takes place for the warrior in which he will receive the Red Feather. This ceremony will not be explained or written in any form and only a veteran with a Red Feather can perform this ceremony. As a result of this ceremony, this veteran has a right to question anyone that wears a red feather. Not just any veteran can wear this red feather. If you have not earned the right to wear the Red Feather, there are harsh consequences, only veterans awarded the Purple Heart during time of war have this right. There is a great responsibility when wearing this feather. With this feather, when called upon to do a task, a red feather veteran must never refuse any task. There is also another ceremony called, "*wase*" (pronounced *wah-say*) or painted [(*wase ikiyu (wah-say ee-kee-yuen)*)] face is only for veterans and this ceremony allows the veteran to paint his face with red paint. This is yet another ceremony and responsibility.

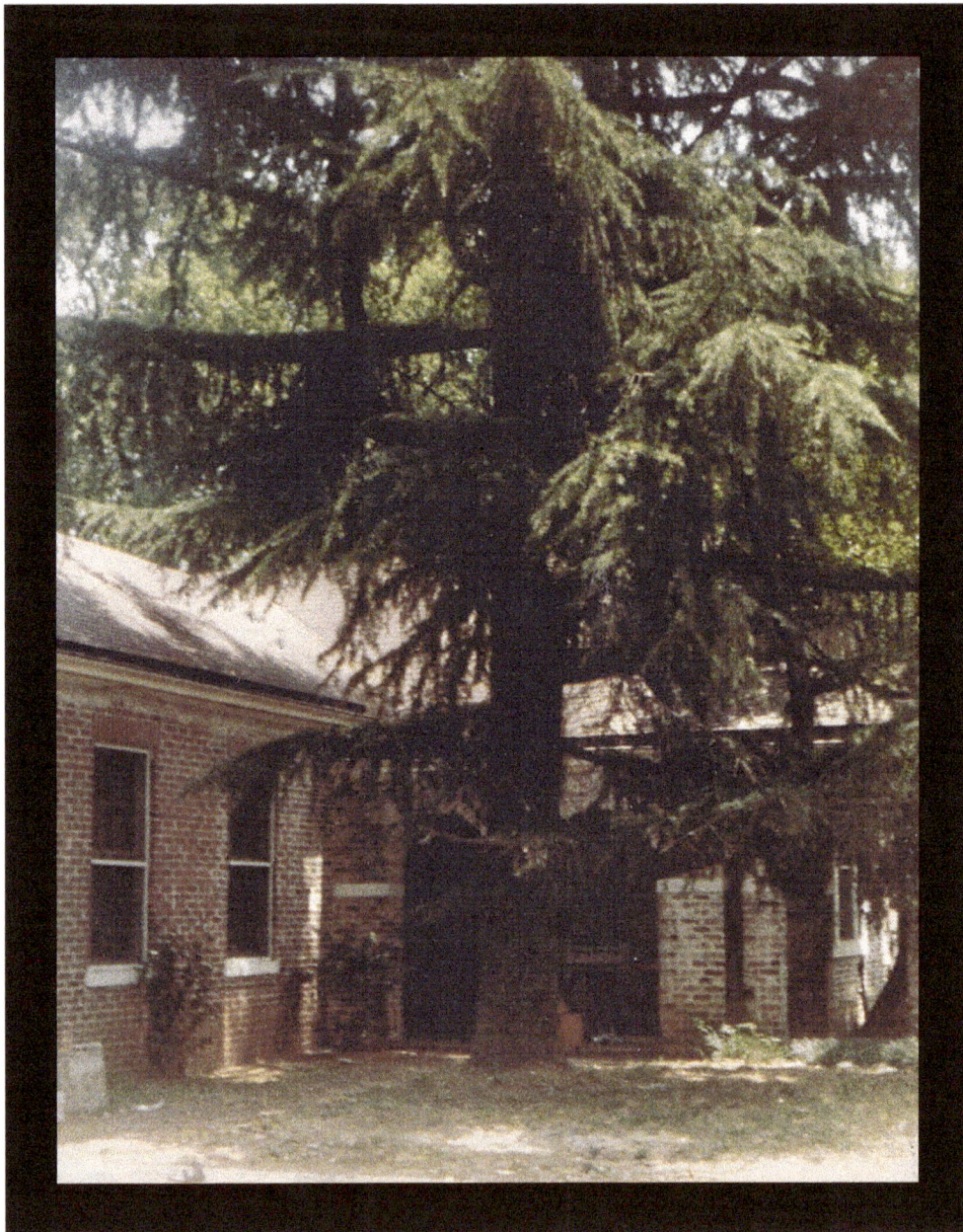

Mercy Home Tree

The little boy's dorm is to the left. Uncle Vernon (house dad) took Ben and another boy in his 1951 Ford to buy a living Christmas tree. It was the first real Christmas tree Ben had ever seen. The boys planted the one and a half foot tree with Uncle Vernon's help. Today the tree towers over the building.

Chapter Two

Mercy

For the first few weeks after being placed in the Mercy Home, Jean missed having her baby sister on her hip. It felt as though something was missing, and it was. The baby was gone but not forgotten. "Even when we asked out mother, she didn't know where she was," recalled Jean. Soon, the three Saxon kids stopped asking about Clyde Dean. They were so caught up in survival that thoughts of their little sister faded.

"We kids were just like a bunch of hopping fleas to the matrons at the Mercy Home," says Jean. "We were irritating and going nowhere." The women of the Red Feather Society had absolutely no expectations of the 65 children in their care, and they made sure the kids knew it. Although they provided for their basic needs – food, clothing and shelter – the matrons seemed to delight in punishing the children in cruel and unusual ways. For instance, three year-old Ben was afraid of dogs because he had never been around them, and when he backed away from a hound in tears one day, he was called a baby in front of the other children. He was then put in a diaper and sent out to the playground. As usual, Ben reacted with anger and filed away that humiliating memory, determined to overcome his fear of dogs. He has since developed a love for all animals, particularly dogs, and now owns two large German Shepherds.

Cute little "cotton-top" that he was, and the youngest of the children there, Ben was often the subject of photographs taken at the Mercy Home. Such was the case during his first Easter Egg Hunt. The photo is a classic because Ben vividly remembers having more concern about being forced to wear a shirt he hated than about finding Easter Eggs.

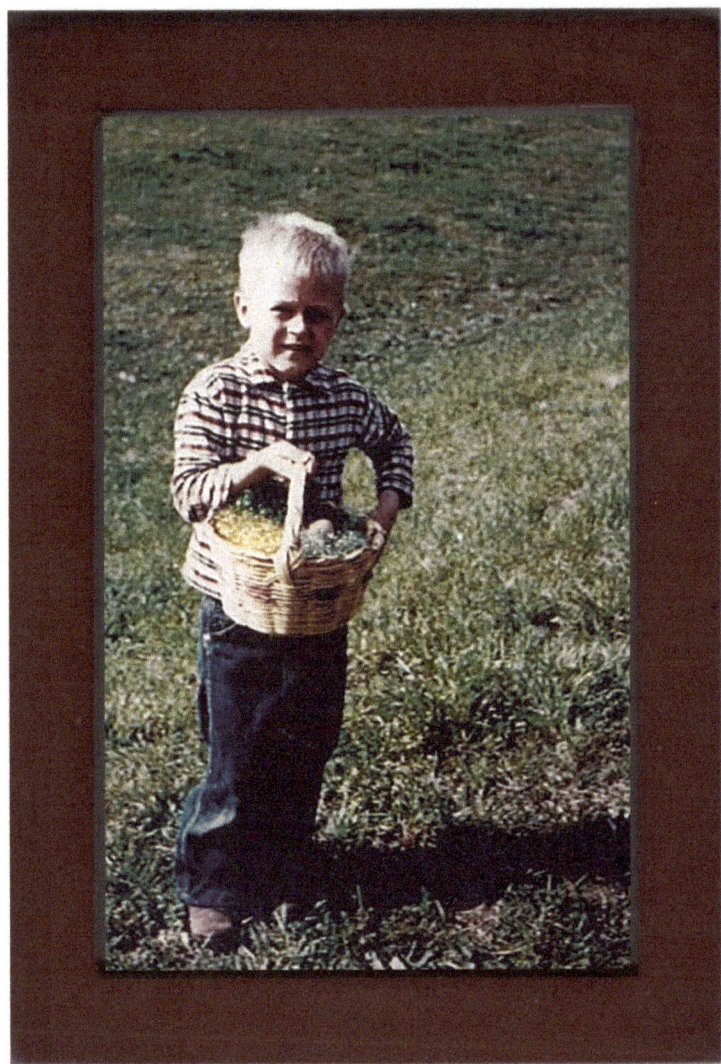

Ben's First Easter Egg Hunt at the Mercy Home (unhappily wearing hated shirt)

While Ben seemed to attract punishment due to his defiant attitude, Jean and Emmett were more careful, doing their best to avoid any negative notice from the matrons. Eventually, despite their efforts, both of them suffered cruel punishment as well. When Emmett and two other boys got caught in some violation – probably foraging for food in the kitchen (as they never quite had enough to eat) – they were forced to wear dresses out on the playground. Emmett laughed about it.

"It was funny to see Emmett in a dress," recalls Jean. "He was almost six feet tall by the time that happened, and everybody laughed at him, so he laughed, too. That's just the way he handled things, but I know it hurt him."

As for Jean, avoiding the suspicious eyes of the matrons – especially the mean one named Inez Hulsey – was a top priority. Jean didn't want to be taken to the clothes closet and paddled (the regular punishment for wayward girls at the Mercy Home), so she did everything in her power to follow the rules. She was paddled only once in that dreaded closet and it was for something she didn't do. "Another girl blamed me for doing something and no matter how hard I tried to deny it, Inez paddled me anyway," she says.

Other than that one paddling, Jean managed to keep her nose clean and do more than what was expected of her. Each of the girls had daily chores to do, but having literally been charged with cooking, cleaning, washing and childcare since she was a toddler, Jean wasn't challenged by the chores at the Mercy Home. Inez was the matron in charge of the girls, and when she observed Jean's work ethic and the fact that she could outwork most of the other girls, she piled even more responsibility on the little girl.

"Inez was a mean old soul," Jean says. "I'm good with numbers and dates and I remember that her birthday was June 5th. Not a June 5th goes by that I don't remember that mean, hollering woman." With her face in a permanent sneer, Inez would instruct Jean to get the sweeper and sweep the living room and make every mark on the carpet perfectly even – or else! Unsmiling and unsympathetic, Inez was the matron in charge when Jean came to the Mercy Home and she was still in that same position seven years later when Jean left.

One of Jean's responsibilities, from early on, was rolling Inez's hair at least once a week. She was told – not asked to do this. She later did hair for a living, but there was never a client she disliked as much as Inez.

Always fascinated with hair, Jean grew up wanting to style others' hair and wishing that someone would make her hair look pretty. She was that little girl of the first grade picture day, whose stringy, unevenly cut hair was kept off her face with a bobby pin … she was also the little girl who daydreamed of having a mother who brushed her clean, soft shining hair each night. By the time she was six, Jean knew that there would be no loving hands washing or brushing her hair. A bit of soap and water every couple of weeks to keep the head-lice at bay was the best she could hope for until coming to the Mercy Home. At least there, she was able to wash her hair and body every day, and she was given a comb to slide through her hair and keep it from sticking up.

At the Mercy home, the Saxon kids ate more regularly than they had ever eaten in their lives, but they were growing children and still never seemed to have enough. There was even a piece of fruit on the table when they got back from school in the afternoon. Jean would eat her banana very slowly because she wanted to make it last. She was always hungry. "We had no choice about what food we ate or how much of it we got on our plate," Jean recalls. There were five girls to a table and everyone had a plate in front of them. A large spoonful of food would be plopped onto the plate, usually four items to a plate, and that was what they had to eat, whether they liked it or not. Jean doesn't remember much meat, but they had

15

macaroni and cheese and canned vegetables and, once in a while, a dessert called Apple Brown Betty. Jean once noticed that there was some left in the serving bowl at dinner and asked for seconds. She was told there wasn't enough for everyone, so she could not have any more. She never asked for seconds again. "I was hungry. We all were. There was never enough food."

One night after they went to their dormitory, did their homework, took their baths and got ready for bed, Jean and several other girls snuck into the kitchen from the back door to get more food. Once there, they were sadly disappointed. Upon opening the door of the huge stainless steel refrigerator, they found it completely empty except for some lemons. The kitchen staff at the Mercy Home had either used up every bit of food available, or it was hidden elsewhere. Still hungry, the girls crept back into the dormitory and slept until 5:30 a.m., when they got dressed, made their beds, ate a breakfast of oatmeal and toast, washed the dishes and walked to the Woodlawn Elementary School. Rain, sleet or snow, the children of the Mercy Home walked the seven long blocks to school. The girls were not allowed to wear slacks and their bare legs suffered in the cold air as they trudged to school, knowing that the Mercy Home's one vehicle – a 1953 Chevrolet Station Wagon with wood on the doors – was in reserve for emergencies only.

Jean had such an emergency when she was ten years old. She was taken to the doctor's office in that 1953 Chevy after falling off of a bicycle and breaking both bones in her right arm. She wore a heavy plaster cast on her right arm for several months and Inez even cut down on some of her chores, but her fifth grade teacher had no sympathy for the little girl from the Mercy Home. She told Jean that she was going to fail if she didn't learn to write with her left hand. Well, Jean took on that challenge as a dare and promptly became ambidextrous. The teachers had low expectations of all the kids at the Mercy Home, but Jean made sure she was an exception. She passed fifth grade easily!

"Nobody thought we were going to amount to anything, anyway," Jean says, "but we knew better. Ben and Emmett and I were determined to get out of the Mercy Home and make something of ourselves – and we did!"

There was a pre-kindergarten area upstairs in the attic of the Mercy Home and Ben's rebellious ways manifested themselves up there when he made a huge mess with finger-paints and conked another kid so hard on the back of his head with a toy gun that he broke the skin. He'd seen cowboys do that and it never happened quite that way in the movies … oh well.

Ben Saxon
Age 6

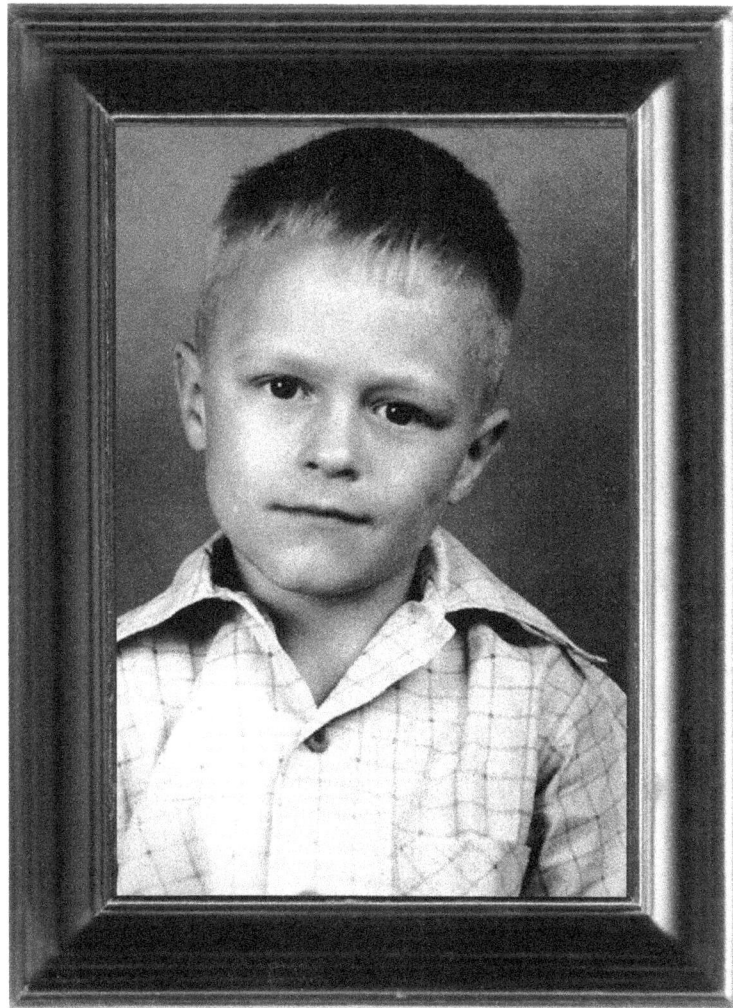

Ben turned six years old on December 5, 1951 and started school on that same day. He was small for his age, but smart and so determined to learn that he caught up with the rest of the class by the end of the year. He had taught himself to read by perusing comic books and reading street signs and when his first grade teacher gave him a B in reading, Ben was mad. He knew he deserved an A. She told him, "You read too fast." He has since learned, as a teacher himself, that some children do read the words without comprehending the meaning, but that was not the case for young Ben Saxon. He knew exactly what he was reading and he knew where he wanted to go with the words ... to the top of the class!

When Ben threatened to run away from the home at age six, no one believed he would do it. He took that disbelief as a direct challenge to his ability and from that moment on, the escape plan was a surety. Convincing another six year old boy to run away with him, Ben and his buddy walked 25 miles across Birmingham, Alabama, across the Viaduct that separated sections of Birmingham, and showed up at the house of the other boy's grandmother. The people at the Mercy Home were furious. They threatened to call the police and have the boys put in jail. "They can't put us in jail. We're not old enough," Ben confidently assured the other boy, as they were being taken back to the home.

Ben was so gutsy that he didn't seem to care about getting in trouble, but it all stemmed from his yearning for some kind of attention to be paid him, even if it was the negative variety. "When I was at the home, I was always looking for some-one to want us, but that didn't happen," Ben recalls. By the time he was seven years old, Ben had overcome his fear of dogs and wanted a puppy in the worst way. He didn't get a puppy at that time, but he was allowed to help the maintenance man with raising rabbits. The rabbits were in a hutch on the far side of a big field behind the little boy's dorm. In the middle of the field, between the dorm and the rabbits, was a large chicken pen where they kept the colored Easter chicks that were donated each year. Corn was grown out there, too, and when someone donated an ostrich, the field became a danger zone. The kids were warned that the ostrich was fast, and could be dangerous. One summer day, Ben was sneaking back from swimming in the nearby stream (which he later found out was a sewer drainage ditch) when he decided to go across the field to the rabbit hutch. Glancing toward the ostrich, he decided, "I can get past that big bird." That day, he did get past the ostrich, just barely – arriving at the fence and jumping over with the big bird hard on his heels.

Another time, while he was supposed to be playing in the school yard at recess, Ben snuck out to the front at lunch time and picked up gravel from the road, throwing handfuls of it at passing cars. When the principal caught him in the act, he grabbed him and yelled, "Don't you dare do that again!" The principal took Ben upstairs to the book room and hit him repeatedly with a little green hose. "Don't – you - ever - think – about - throwing – rocks - at - a - car - again!" he yelled, emphasizing each word with a swat of the hose. The next chance Ben got, he went right back out and did it again. This time, he didn't get caught, so he eventually stopped doing it. It wasn't fun anymore.

A scientifically-oriented loner at an early age, Ben often spent time out on the physical education field collecting bugs rather than participating in team sports. With the exception of his siblings, Ben found that he liked and trusted animals more than he did people, and with good reason. He was withdrawn, not because he was shy but because he preferred not to converse. There were Vespers every Sunday night and sometimes people would send him home with a family for the weekend. They were strangers to Ben. "People would talk to me and I wouldn't say anything more than I had to," he remembers. "I wanted someone to really care, but I didn't think any of them did."

With one daredevil stunt after another, Ben did his best to get attention, but the one person from whom he yearned for attention was his mother, who was incapable of giving him what he wanted. "Mother did not know her children," he says. "She was never around us that much, but for some reason, she said repeatedly that she didn't want her boys to be adopted." Ben learned much later that the minister at church had approached his mother and the home about adopting him and that Emily's mother had wanted to adopt a boy and a girl and had been willing to adopt one of her brothers. It was ironic that at the same time his mother was refusing to sign adoption papers, Ben and his sister, Jean, were dreaming of being wanted and loved and having a real family. God has a way of working things out, though, as Emmett would probably have been left behind, and his sister and brother were the only family he knew or wanted.

Although separated by age and gender, the siblings occasionally caught glimpses of one another at meals, on walks to school, and on the playground, but rarely were they allowed any quality time together. One day, the matron instructed Jean to go help her little brother, Ben, with math homework. Excited, Jean went to Ben's dorm to help him, but when she got there, he had already done it. "I'm not going to be a ditch digger," seven-year old Ben told her, squaring his jaw and gritting his teeth. "I'm going to college." Smart, determined and worldly at an extremely young age, Ben defiantly tested the limits and instigated disobedience of the Mercy Home rules at every opportunity.

On Sundays, Ben and Emmett were allowed to walk to church together. Sometimes, they would take the nickel they'd been given for the collection plate and buy cigarettes instead. Emmett would sit behind the store and smoke. Ben tried it and didn't like it, but he went along with his brother anyway. Once in a while, when they actually did go to church, they would first sneak up to the Sunday school social area where there were couches and cold drinks in a large tub filled with ice. They'd quick grab a bottle of coke but in order to get into the church service in time, they'd have to chugalug it down fast. Then Ben would be so bloated with gas from the fizz that his stomach would hurt. Rarely did they make it through an entire church service without having to take a quick trip to the bathroom. "You were supposed to leave a dime for a bottle of coke, but we never did, and no one ever said anything," recalls Ben. "People felt sorry for us." One day, for instance, Ben was walking on the sidewalk when a car pulled up and the window was rolled

19

down. A lady stuck her hand out the window and said, "Here little boy, would you like half of my candy bar?" It was a Mounds Bar and Ben took it – he knew Jean would love it. But it was hot outside so he had to eat it before it melted.

Ben helped Jean and Emmett whenever he could. Even though he was the youngest of the three, he had an innate sensitivity that gave him a caregiver's heart. Jean had that same compassionate love for her siblings, but Emmett had somehow had the sensitivity knocked out of him at an early age. He was quiet and appeared to be a deep thinker, but was often just daydreaming. When approached by anyone, Emmett would just smile as if he didn't have a care in the world.

Emmett wanted to do right, but was not willing to take a chance on putting himself out if there was risk involved. He lived in his own world and did his own thing. There was also an underlying resentment in him toward Ben. His younger brother was so quick to learn, and, through no fault of his own, Emmett found that school-work was difficult for him. Later in life, Emmett finally found his niche as a long-distance truck driver. He grew up to be a good man who, like his siblings, went out of his way to help people and worked hard to support his family.

Emmett Saxon, Jr. – about age 8

When Ben was in second grade, he was one of the few students who could look at a clock and tell what time it was. He wanted a watch in the worst way, but he didn't get one until many years later, when he was 14 years old and bought a pocket watch from his cousin for a dollar. Ben and his siblings were accustomed to wanting and not getting. They had no toys or treasured possessions. They clung to whatever they were given and took nothing for granted. Until the Mercy Home, Christmas had been non-existent for the Saxon kids. Holidays meant nothing to people like their parents who were living hand to mouth and barely knew what day it was.

At the Mercy Home, some semblance of Christmas did exist. Jean remembers that they would get stockings filled with oranges and nuts – none of the sweet candy that she yearned for – and then they would all gather around a large Christmas tree piled high with wrapped presents. The matrons would pick up a gift and read the tag. "This is for a girl," they would announce, or "This is for a boy." Indiscriminately, they passed presents around to the girls and boys, with no thought given to their age or wishes. Jean, too, wanted a watch, but never got one. She remembers one Christmas when she opened her gift to find a miniature china tea set – obviously second-hand. It was a gift that was less than useless to a teenaged girl. "A tea set wasn't what I wanted – I knew that for sure," she recalls, "but then, I didn't know enough about having things to even know what I did want."

Ben seemed to always know what he wanted to possess and he went after it, whether it was for Christmas or any other occasion. He had seen scissors at school and was fascinated by the way they cut things. He let it be known, loudly, that he wanted a pair of scissors for Christmas. His mother came for a rare Christmas visit that year. Ben was in 2nd grade and he and Emmett got to go home with their mother for the day.

Christine and Pop went in together and got Ben his scissors - a tiny pair with red plastic on the handle. Ben was so excited. He was holding his new scissors in one hand and fingering the vinyl cloth underneath the telephone table in the hallway with the other hand when his mother noticed. "You touch that and I'm going to beat your butt!" she threatened. He cut the table cloth with his new scissors as soon as she walked in the door of the apartment. Sure enough, she came out and caught him at it and beat his butt. He never saw those scissors again.

While his little brother struggled with unfulfilled desires and tested the boundaries at every turn, young Emmett Saxon escaped into his own world of oblivion – not expecting anything and thus never being disappointed when he didn't get anything. He was quiet and pleasant and just somehow drifted along, barely making it in school and rarely catching the eye of the matrons at the Mercy Home. All Emmett ever wanted was a family – people who loved him and cared for him – and that family was represented by his sister, Jean, and his brother, Ben. He knew they would always be there for him, and that's all he needed. He had no agenda and no particular goals, except to please his siblings and make them proud of him. Emmett knew, without any question, that the main goal of their little family of three was to grow up and become productive adults. "We Saxons had a thing to do," says Jean. "We were going to be somebody."

Ben made almost straight A's throughout elementary school, although his 4th grade teacher (Ms. Sharp) warned him that his brain was working faster than his hand and he was making too many written mistakes. He didn't forget that warning, and applied it to his future learning. There were a few mentors along the way, including the couple at the Mercy Home (house parents) called Aunt Hattie and Uncle Vernon. They would occasionally take in four or five of the boys who didn't go home on weekends. That generally included Ben and Emmett. At Aunt Hattie and Uncle Vernon's house, the boys would sleep on the floor and awake to the smell of pancakes. Once in a while, life was just right, and those pancake mornings somehow helped create some sort of balance for the boys, but nothing substituted for hugs – and hugs were something not meted out to any of the children at the Mercy Home. No hugs – no kisses. It took many years for Ben, in particular, to feel comfortable with hugs and kisses. He realized, as a young adult, how foreign it was for him to display affection. His grandchildren now reap the benefits of that realization, as he generously hands out hugs and kisses to them whenever he can.

Ben was in 5th grade when he had his first crush on a girl. Jane Mitchell lived in the girl's dorm at the Mercy Home and she would walk back and forth to school with Ben. One day, Ben tried to get Jane's attention by throwing a rock through the window of the girl's dorm. "It was a pebble, really," says Ben, "but I threw it hard enough to crack the window." The screen and window were taken down and Ben was sent to the repair shop to have them fixed. The man who fixed the screen and window obviously liked the story and the boy … he gave Ben 50 cents in addition to the repaired window and screen. Ben bought candy and a cold drink with it, and saved the candy and drink to give to Emmett and Jean on Saturday, movie night. That movie night, they watched the movie "Don't Fence Me In," and Jane was there watching it, too.

"Ben Lee was the first boy that was ever sweet to me and I've never for-gotten it," recalls Jane today, some five-plus decades later. A married woman who lives in Palatka, Florida, Jane has always wanted to find Ben and thank him for his kindness.

In a classic case of "the rest of the story," it turns out that Jane's son-in-law, David Trzeciak, was a student of Ben's in Ocala and when he heard his mother-in-law talking about her first love, Ben Lee Saxon, he put two and two together. Through David, Ben and Jane met again after all those years and talked for hours about old times when they were both "throw-away kids" at the Mercy Home. It was a good reunion, but as Ben says, firmly, "You can never go back."

Jane Mitchell – age 11

Although Jane called him sweet, Ben was not a boy who liked sweets. Whenever he got candy, he gave it to his siblings. "I'm not a sweets person," he admits, leaving the double meaning hanging in the wake of his words. Whether or not he enjoyed eating sweets, though, Ben Saxon somehow managed to do sweet giving acts for his sister and brother whenever he could. He saved the Sugar Easter Eggs with the scene in them and gave them to his siblings. He shopped for them at Woolworth's with his 35 cent allowance and the $5 he was allowed to spend on a gift by the 10th of December until he turned ten. He bought a Peter Pan doll for Jean and Christmas presents for his brother and his mother whenever he could.

When a horse was donated to the Mercy Home, the children were all excited about the possibility of riding. A lady was hired to take care of the horse and one day Jean was watching the lady lead the horse around the building when the horse leaned over and bit into the muscle of the lady's arm, breaking the skin and causing the lady great anguish. Since that day, Jean has been afraid of horses. She has

23

never ridden one and has no desire to be around them at all, despite the fact that Ben enjoys riding and has urged her often to overcome that fear. "I don't like horses and I never will," she says stubbornly. "My mind was made up that day I saw the horse bite the lady."

Jean has always had her mind firmly made up about many things, one being that she preferred being alone to being involved in the problems represented by the other girls at the Mercy Home. Jean would get her chores done and then curl up alone with a book. There were a limited number of books at the Mercy Home, most of them for young children, but Jean read every one of them. The girls would sometimes sneak comic books like "Jughead" into the dorm and hide them under the mattresses so the matron wouldn't find them. Among the books available to her at the Mercy home, Aesop's Fables were her favorites and she read them over and over again. The morals and lessons taught in those fables have stayed with her all her life. Some of those fables that helped her become the woman she is today were: *The Tortoise & The Hare* (Perseverance), *The Friends & The Bear* (Friendship), *The Crow & the Pitcher* (Ingenuity and Hard Work), *The Boy That Cried Wolf* (Honesty), *The Father's Bundle* (Family), and *The Lion and The Mouse* (Everyone needs kindness and help).

At school, the librarian opened her up to a larger world of books. She would read classic fairy tales to the students as Jean sat in rapt attention, listening to every word the librarian read. Jean devoured each book she could get her hands on in the library. Reading became even more enjoyable after she got her school eye test and the home was notified that she needed glasses. Jean has been wearing glasses since she was 11 years old. Her glasses are an integral part of her wardrobe, and they help her continue to enjoy reading books daily.

At the Mercy Home, kids were not allowed to take books out to the playground. When it was time to go out and play, Jean sat alone, leaning against the far wall and using her imagination as she played with the rocks she found on the playground. "I took those rocks and built things with them. I made a dream house and a car and let my imagination run wild, pretending this was my house and a normal family was living there – with a mom and dad, somebody scrambling my eggs and helping me get dressed for school in the morning and about to drive me to school – just a normal, everyday family." It was what Jean prayed for every night before she went to sleep, but it was only a dream that seemed hopeless.

When her Sunday School teacher, Mrs. Denby, took Jean home after church sometimes, Jean saw a bit of what a normal home life must be. Mrs. Denby was childless and she must have seen something special in Jean to take her home. Lunch at Mrs. Denby's was great because Jean would get enough to eat for a change, but even if she wanted more, she had learned never to ask for seconds. "You come to a point where you don't ask, but when Mrs. Denby would ask if I wanted some more, I'd always say 'Yes, ma'am!'"

There were kind people like Mrs. Denby all along the way, and Jean remembers their kindnesses, but mostly she remembers feeling alone and abandoned. Pop, (grandpa) who always walked wherever he went, no matter how far, sometimes came to visit his three grandkids at the Mercy Home. His visits were rare and he didn't stay long, as he was facing a long walk back home, but the fact that he came was so important to the three Saxon kids. They loved their Pop very much.

Ben vividly remembers one day when the three of them were visiting their mother, who was living in an old-fashioned duplex at the time with a little country store at the front of the property. "Emmett, Jean and I were there when Pop came by and took us into that little store and bought us each ten cent boxes of Crackerjacks. Then he bought us another box and another box. You had to finish the Crackerjacks to get to the prize at the bottom of the box. We ate Crackerjacks until we all got sick as dogs. It was one of the few times in my childhood when I remember getting as much as I wanted of something … and then when I did, it made me sick!"

While her siblings were so starved for food and affection that they didn't know what to do with it when they got it, their little sister, Clyde Dean (Emily), was living in what they would have considered a dream world. At about the same time Jean, Ben and Emmett were eating their fill of Crackerjacks, Emmaline was enjoying picnics at her family's own private lake outside of Anniston, Alabama. "Daddy and Mama and another couple went in together and bought lake property when I was about seven years old," she recalls. "We'd go out there on a Friday or Saturday night and have fish fries, with hush puppies and all the fixings. One lady always made the best caramel cake. I'll never forget how good that tasted!" Sometimes her daddy would take her fishing for catfish or brim (bream) out on the lake in his john boat. "He couldn't get me to be quiet when we were out there fishing!" she recalls, laughing. "Ben says he's not surprised about that because I still won't be quiet!"

An only child, Emmaline grew up with many cousins, aunts and uncles and an annual family reunion where everyone caught up with everyone's latest news. She loved parties and gatherings and always had a birthday party with a cake and games and friends. Her sixth birthday was especially memorable, as it was her first birthday party in her new "forever home."

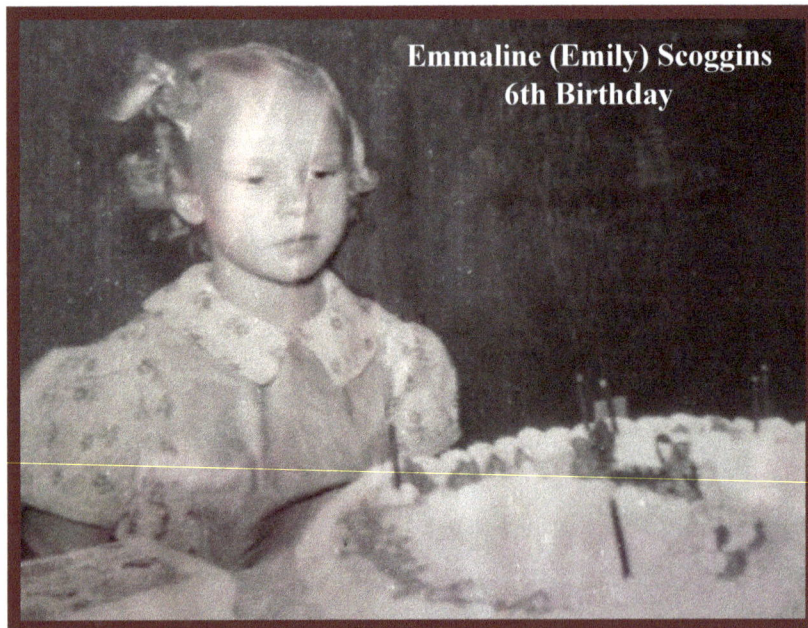
Emmaline (Emily) Scoggins
6th Birthday

One family story on Emmaline, at about 7 or 8 years old, was the time when she simply decided she wanted to have a party and proceeded to go from door to door in her Anniston neighborhood, telling the neighbors that she was having a party that night and inviting them to come to her house. Then she went home and told her Mama to get everything ready because they were having a party. "She gave me a talking-to about that one!" Emmaline remembers. "Luckily, no believed me and so no one came to the party that night."

Yes, Emmaline was loved. She lived an idyllic life with two doting parents and surrounded by family who found her adorable, but back at the Mercy Home, Jean, Emmett and Ben were not adored. Receiving the bare minimum of institutional care – a roof over their heads, clothes on their backs, a bed to sleep in and food to eat – the three Saxon kids learned early that love was not part of the Mercy Home's services.

Once in a great while, their mother would visit, but she was more like a distant relative or friend than a mother. There were two photos taken of Christine and her kids on a rare visiting day – one with her three children, Emmett leaning back on the fence with his shirt-tail out, Ben looking thoughtful – his hand on his face and his shirt tucked in, pants neatly belted, and Jean, appearing distracted and pensive, standing next to her mother. Christine is smiling, but she does not touch any of her children in the photograph – simply stands in the midst of them, holding hands with no one on either side. Hugging and kissing was not something the Saxon kids got from their mother, or anyone else. They were not taught to display physical affection when they were growing up and, even today, it is not easy for them to be demonstrative, even when they are filled with love for one another, or for children and grandchildren. "You have to learn that at home, and we didn't have it," says Jean.

To be fair, Christine had never received physical affection at home when she was growing up, so how could she pass it on to her children? Her mother died young and left Pop with six kids, Christine being the oldest girl and the one charged with taking care of the rest. There was neither time nor reason for hugging and kissing. Just living day by day was the main thing. Christine learned early on to look out for herself first. Being self-centered was how she survived.

The other photo, of Jean and her mother, is in front of a wall at the Mercy Home – possibly the same wall that Jean leaned against while she built her rock fantasies of home, car and family. In that photo, even though they are standing close to one another, mother and daughter are not touching. "We just were told to get cleaned up – our mother was there. So we did," notes Jean. "We didn't know her that much as we were growing up. She was always looking for somebody to take care of her, and so were we. She had no education and she had no motherly instincts."

Jean wore her new teal dress with the little figures on it that day she and her mother posed for the photo. One of the matrons had made it for her … definitely not Inez! Jean scoffs at the thought of Inez actually making a dress for someone. "She couldn't make up her mind what day it was, let alone make a dress!" Jean jokes, with a somewhat bitter tone to her voice. Jean, posing prettily beside her mother, had a neat figure and was wearing high heels that made them the same height. It wasn't long after this photo was taken that Jean, at age 15, aged out of the Mercy Home and moved in with a foster family.

Leaving the Mercy Home for a foster home was a big step for Jean. As she set out for her new life, she made a silent vow to herself. "When I leave here, I will never be cold or hungry again." She has kept that vow.

Chapter Three

Fosters

After nearly seven years at the Mercy Home, Jean Saxon couldn't wait to get out. At 15, she was slim, pretty and well-behaved, a quiet girl who wasn't afraid of hard work and didn't need to be entertained. She could spend hours by herself reading books. Jean was eager to please her foster mother, Bessie Murphree, and at her request, called her Aunt Bessie. Bessie and Virdo Murphree, an older couple who took in foster children for the money, had several fosters, including Jean, living in their small three-bedroom house. "She had bunches of us in one room, but it wasn't bad living there," Jean recalls. "I learned a lot watching Aunt Bessie in the kitchen, and asking questions, and if I was hungry, I just went in and fixed it." Aunt Bessie and Uncle Virdo didn't fuss at Jean or fight with one another. Bessie made biscuits for Virdo every morning and Jean watched as he put syrup and butter on them. It was a friendly family kind of thing to do, and Jean was starved for family.

When Jean got there, she had quite a few clothes that had been given to her by Mrs. Denby. Bessie Murphree had a daughter about ten years older than Jean who was married and had a child. "Why don't you give Mary Belle some of those clothes?" Bessie asked Jean, but Jean resisted. Bessie didn't pressure her and Jean kept her clothes. They were the only things she owned and who knew when she'd get more.

The only big problem with the Murphrees was that they attended the Church of God of Prophecy on Wednesdays and Sundays and, if there was a revival going on, they went every day. They spoke in tongues at the church and it was uncomfortable for Jean. "I was out the door of that church as soon as I was able," she recalls. "It gave me the creeps." Occasionally, Aunt Bessie would invite Emmett and Ben to spend the weekend with them, which the boys truly appreciated ... except for having to attend that what they considered that "crazy" church. Ben remembers that they would have to go with the family, but would crawl out under the pews as quickly as possible. Mrs. Denby's Methodist Church was much more to Jean's liking, and that of her brothers, as well. Jean has been a Methodist ever since she had the decision-making power in her own hands.

During the nearly three years she was with the Murphrees, Jean was just biding her time, attending Hewitt Trussville High School, missing her brothers, and wishing for something better. Her grades in high school were just passing, but she did have a burning goal and that was to be a hairdresser. She would eventually attend cosmetology school and become a licensed hairdresser, but her first desire was to have a family of her own. When she met a boy in high school that she was attracted to, she decided this might be the way to start her own family – by marrying him. Jean was 17 years old when she got married, and it didn't take her long to discover that she'd made a mistake.

While Jean worked 18 hours a day at a restaurant, her new husband stayed in bed all day and all night. Jean wanted to get pregnant and start her family. She thought if she had a baby, he'd get out of bed and go out and find a job, but it didn't work that way at all. They moved in with his parents when she was about six months pregnant and what she remembers most vividly about her mother-in-law was that she made biscuits that were as hard as hockey pucks. His parent's home was a drafty old wood house and, while Jean was pregnant and living there, she came down with double pneumonia. She gave birth to her son, Bruce on May 25, 1959 and soon thereafter she got a divorce for $75, and went back to work in a restaurant.

In the meantime, Emmett had aged out of the Mercy Home at age 14 in 1957 and Ben, at 11 ½, decided he wanted to leave with his brother. Along with Sherman, another boy aging out of the Mercy Home, Emmett and Ben had gone to live in a foster home in Morris, Alabama. "I just knew there had to be something better than the Mercy Home out there, and I was determined to find it," recalls Ben.

As foster kids, the three boys were supposed to be helping their foster-parent, Mr. Peyton, on his farm because he was getting too old to do the farm work himself. They did farm chores as requested but Ben remembers that sometimes Sherman and Emmett would go into the woods and disappear for hours at a time. There was a mule at the Peyton farm and Emmett jumped on his back and got thrown into the strawberry patch. Some of that innate Saxon determination came out when he got thrown. He kept getting back on the mule until he finally rode him.

Speaking of riding, the Peytons (through welfare) gave the three boys a used bike that first Christmas they were living with them. One bike between three boys was a challenge, but they did their best to share it, albeit reluctantly. Soon, that problem was solved. The bike got a flat tire and the Peyton's were not willing to fix it.

Mrs. Peyton was head of the cafeteria at the high school and every day, the school bus dropped them off where she worked. For the first time in Ben's memory, food was not a main issue. They ate pretty well at the Peyton's house and he was gratified to find that Mrs. Peyton loved to cook French fries. French fries were then, and still are, one of Ben's favorite foods.

By the time they were in foster care, Ben had caught up with Emmett scholastically and both of them entered the same 6th grade class in Morris, Alabama. Because they were known by all to be poor foster kids, the boys were required to pay for their lunch by emptying the garbage. They had to carry it all the way across the baseball field, which was quite a struggle for a kid Ben's size, and he resented every step he took across that field. While Emmett and Sherman could have cared less about school, Ben put his nose to the grindstone and, as always, worked hard at his studies. It was rough going in the little country school, but he made it through the year with perfect attendance. When the teacher, Ms. Moseley, asked a question, Ben always had the answer to it. This irritated the other students and didn't set well with the teacher either.

"We were just foster kids. We weren't supposed to be smart. Ms. Moseley ignored us mostly," Ben remembers. "She put me towards the back of the room." Ben wasn't surprised at this undeserved treatment. He had experienced something similarly hurtful in 5th grade, when his teacher, Mrs. Oliver, had purposely eliminated him from winning the spelling bee. The spelling contest had come down to Ben and a girl whose family was there to cheer her on. The deciding word was "envelope," which Ben spelled correctly and the girl spelled without the "e" at the end of the word. The teacher announced that Ben had spelled the word incorrectly and the girl was the winner of the contest. The girl's family cheered loudly and the teacher smiled. "Mrs. Oliver knew that I knew the truth, and it didn't matter. I thought to myself, 'The teacher's right, I'm wrong. What the heck! I'm defeated, and nobody cares." He wasn't supposed to win that contest. That was a hard pill for Ben to swallow … that no matter how smart he was or how hard he worked, nobody really cared. He quietly internalized that knowledge and worked even harder to excel, because he came to the realization that somebody really did care … and that somebody was Ben Saxon.

Although there was no spelling bee in 6th grade in Morris, Alabama, there was some sort of competition where everyone in the class won a ballpoint pen. Ben was so proud of his new pen. He'd never had a pen of his own. Then a girl in the class began crying because someone had taken her pen. It had a mark on it and Ben was accused of taking it. Somebody had switched her pen with Ben's and, basically, framed him as the perpetrator. "They made a big deal about what a thief I was," he remembers, "and I've never had to steal anything in my life." What hurt Ben even more than being accused of stealing was the fact that his brother, Emmett, knew exactly what had happened, and didn't defend or stand up for him. "Emmett sat right there and didn't say one word. He was afraid to say anything."

At school, in addition to being looked down on and wrongly accused of things they didn't do, Emmett, Ben and the other foster-boy, Sherman, were expected to do other janitorial services in addition to the garbage detail. They were not supposed to tell anybody they were cleaning bathrooms and floors, as Mr. Peyton got paid extra for their services and it was not part of the foster care program, so they did their work on weekends and holidays when no one was there to see them. One Friday night before a holiday, the boys decided to clean the school early so that they wouldn't have to be there during their time out of school. When they got home and Mr. Peyton asked Ben about their lateness, he didn't offer an explanation because he didn't want to get in trouble. He got in trouble anyway because, they said, he didn't tell them the truth right away. Ben admits that he did have a self-confident air about him that irritated the people in charge. That self-confident act was his wall that protected him against expressing himself in anger and tears when he was treated like a second-class citizen. Unfortunately, once in a great while he would let his guard down and mouth a defiant remark. That was what did him in at the Peyton's.

"Mrs. Peyton had asthma and she was always cooking that vapor stuff in a tin pie plate at the stove," recalls Ben. "One day she was standing at the stove when we came in the kitchen and she yelled that she was tired of us making a mess and making so much noise. I said, 'If you don't like it, we can just leave.' She called welfare and had us picked up within days."

Ms. Robinson, the welfare lady, sent Emmett and Ben to their mother and step-father. At the time, their mother and her husband, Travis Sloan, lived in a half duplex with a gas station next door near Birmingham, Alabama. Travis, a one-armed man with a drinking problem and a bad temper, had an ax to grind from the beginning. He didn't want to have anything to do with Christine's children. He always told her that he wasn't raising his own kids and he wasn't going to raise hers. When the boys arrived, he told them, "I'm going to put you out there to pick weeds along the fence and the one who does the best job gets to stay." Ben had the dubious honor of getting to stay.

Welfare put Emmett in another foster home, but by that time, he was nearly 16 years old and it wasn't long before he left foster care and reconnected with his big sister, Jean, who had been trying to find her brothers. Jean, by then divorced with a baby, needed Emmett desperately. He moved in with her and took care of her son, Bruce, while she worked at the truck stop and supported the three of them.

Ben started 7th grade in a school about two miles from where his mother and her husband lived. While most kids are taken to school to get registered and get their books and their class assignments, Ben simply appeared there and registered himself. His mother and her husband could have cared less whether he attended school or not, but Ben cared very much. He walked back and forth to school every day and worked hard to make good grades. One day on the way to school, he found a little puppy and let it follow him home. Travis took an instant dislike to it and the puppy stayed out in the back yard on a chain, eating whatever scraps Ben could spare, as buying dog food was out of the question.

Soon, Ben's mother and her husband moved to Leesburg, Florida to live with Uncle Johnny (Christine's brother) and his girlfriend. Pop was also living there, which made six people when Christine, Travis and Ben moved in. Sometime during the time they were at Uncle Johnny's and Ben was at school, Ben's pup was killed when his Uncle Johnny threw a pop bottle at it because it was bringing a dead bird home in its mouth. All he said to Ben was, "The puppy is dead cause' I don't want any dead birds around my house."

It was Ben's first puppy and he has never forgotten the sadness of its death.

In the spring of 1958, they moved to Ocala. There, they lived out at Roosevelt Village, which had been an old military barracks. Once again, Ben registered himself for 7th grade at the school in Ocala. He finished his 7th grade year only because most of what he studied he had already had in Alabama. Ashamed of where and how he lived, Ben was determined to rise above it and somehow bring respect to the name "Saxon" in that close-knit and often close-minded community. He knew he was an excellent speller and when the county-wide spelling bee came up, he entered after being at the school less than a week. Ben made a good showing, coming in third. He was proud of himself for being up on that stage and being the third best in the county until he learned that the boy who won (the privileged son of highly respected citizens in Ocala) had been given a list of words to study prior to the spelling bee! It was a prime example of the "haves and have nots," but despite it all, Ben Saxon had amazed everyone by being unexpectedly up on that stage in his torn clothes and old beach shoes. Placing in that fixed competition meant a great deal to him.

About three quarters of the way through 8th grade in Ocala, Ben's mother and her husband took him out of school and told him they were going to visit Uncle Hoyt in Alabama. After a day or two at Hoyt's, they drove off, leaving Ben there. "They dumped me and left without saying a word," he remembers. Uncle Hoyt and his wife, Liz, had their own four kids. He was just another mouth to feed. Somehow, Ben did finish 8th grade there, but in August of the following summer, Liz took him to some friends of theirs, the Sykes, and said, "You can have him. We don't want him."

Ben stayed with the Sykes family for nine weeks, beginning 9th grade at the school near McDonald's Chapel, Alabama. But the Sykes family didn't want him either. Welfare picked him up and took him to the Mercy Home as a last resort until they could find someplace for him. There, he had a roof over his head but didn't go to school. He stayed and did physical work for the home until just before Christmas when they put him on a Greyhound bus and sent him back to his mother's shack in Ocala.

"I hated being a kid – hated being nobody – hated the way people treated me," declares Ben, tasting once again the bitterness he felt when shunted from home to home and then forced to walk back into the bad situation in Ocala. Christmas came and went. The abuse from Travis intensified.

"Get him out of here!" Travis yelled one day in response to something Ben had muttered under his breath. "It was my smart mouth," Ben admits. "I controlled it with everybody else, but when it came to my mother's husband, sometimes I just had to respond to the meanness."

Ben was in 9th grade at Ocala Junior High School when the level of abuse at his mother's place got so bad that welfare was once again forced to step in and place him elsewhere. In February of 1961, a well-to-do family in Ocala took Ben in as a foster child.

While Ben was being thrown from one bad situation into the next, Jean had finally applied for and gotten custody of Emmett, who was soon to age out of the system anyway. Emmett took care of little Bruce while Jean worked long hours at a restaurant. They moved around to where the jobs were for Jean – and they lived in Mississippi and in Philadelphia, and elsewhere. By then they had reconnected with their mother and their brother, Ben, in Ocala, and that was where they were when Jean walked into a little restaurant at Raney's Truck Stop, where a handsome man named Harry Acree worked. Harry was a former coal miner from West Virginia – a hard worker, a good man with a kind heart. "I had my son, Bruce, and my brother, Emmett, with me, and I was looking for work," she recalls. "I didn't like the restaurant, but I did like Harry."

Soon, Jean and Harry were sharing RC Colas and Moon Pies together, and it wasn't long before Harry asked Jean to marry him. Harry Acree was the love of Jean's life. He immediately adopted three-year old Bruce. "He loved Bruce as much as he loved me, if not more," says Jean. Emmett continued living with the Acrees, despite the fact that they were dirt-poor and just getting by. Harry was generous not only with his wallet, but with his heart. He taught his young brother-in-law a great deal about truck maintenance and repair and gave him some good direction on what would eventually become Emmett's life-long career of driving trucks cross-country.

Meanwhile, in a life far away from the harsh reality experienced by her long-lost siblings, young Emmaline Sarah Scoggins was growing up in a loving home as an only child adored by her parents. Her father and his brother-in-law owned a hardware store in Anniston, Alabama and she would come by the store and spend time in the tool section. As a girl, she loved the smell of hardware. The bins of nails and screws and all of the metal and wooden tools fascinated her. She, like her big sister, Jean, also loved sweets. Her father would often bring home candy from the store and her mother would protest, but he'd sneak her some M&M's when Mama wasn't looking.

In 1959, when Jean was giving birth to Bruce and her brothers, Emmett and Ben, were in and out of foster care in Morris, Alabama and elsewhere, Clyde Dean (Emmaline/Emily) was ten years old. Her father got a new job with a cement company that year and the family moved to Vicksburg, Mississippi, where Emmaline was destined to attend elementary, junior high and high school, graduating in 1966. She would meet her future husband, Roger Mullings, in high school and, after he joined the Navy and spent some time in Turkey, Emmaline and Roger would get married in Ragland, Alabama in January 1967.

"Many times, over the years, we were physically close – in the same town or county – to our little sister, Emily, but we didn't know it at the time," says Ben. "Emily knew she was adopted, but had no memory of us. We never forgot her, of course, and later, we learned from our mother that she had given birth to another little girl in 1951 (Paula Woodall Manning) and left her at the hospital to go into the foster care system. She always called that baby "Little Debbie," just as she talked of our sister, Clyde Dean (Emmaline/Emily) as "Rickie." Those lost daughters became more and more important to our mother as she got older. She begged us, especially me, to find them and bring all of her five children together again."

Ben and Jean searched for years for their lost sisters, sending out more than 500 letters. Ben finally hired a private detective who found them in 1985. Ben was, and is, one determined person who sets his mind to something and achieves it, despite all challenges. That determination served him well in 9th grade, when he went from being a ragged, abused kid living in a tarpaper shack to being a Page in Washington, D.C.

Chapter four

Capitol Page

Mr. Tinsley, Ben's 9th grade Civics teacher at Ocala Junior High, invited a speaker to come to the school and talk about his experience as a Capitol Page in Washington, D.C. "I'm going to do that," decided Ben, writing a letter to Florida Congressman Albert S. Herlong, Jr. that very day.

Ben, being a foster child with nothing but the clothes on his back, got quite a bit of notoriety in Ocala when he was chosen to go to Washington, D.C. as a Congressional Page. The Ocala newspaper even put a picture of Ben in the paper. Ben looks at it today and notes that he looks like a poor little orphan boy in his ragged, ill-fitting clothing, and that the reporter for the paper even paraphrased Ben's comment, writing that the boy had said he was "thrilled" (not a word Ben would ever choose). What Ben had actually told the reporter was that he was happy to be able to serve his country at his age.

Ben Saxon, 15, of Anthony Road, has been appointed to serve as Page in the House of Representatives in the nation's capitol by Congressman Syd Herlong.

In Herlong's letter to young Saxon, dated April 17, the congressman informed him that he was to report to Washington on May 1, to assume his duties in the House.

Saxon, who will serve throughout May as Herlong's messenger, stated that he wrote three letters to the congressman asking for the position before being accepted this past week.

A ninth grade student at Ocala Junior High, Ben's ambition is to enter the University of Florida and receive a degree for a career as a teacher.

Presently working as a news carrier for the Star-Banner, Saxon regards English as his favorite subject in school.

"It was really a thrill to be appointed by Mr. Herlong and I look forward to May 1. I am honored that I was chosen and I shall try my best to be a good page," the boy said..

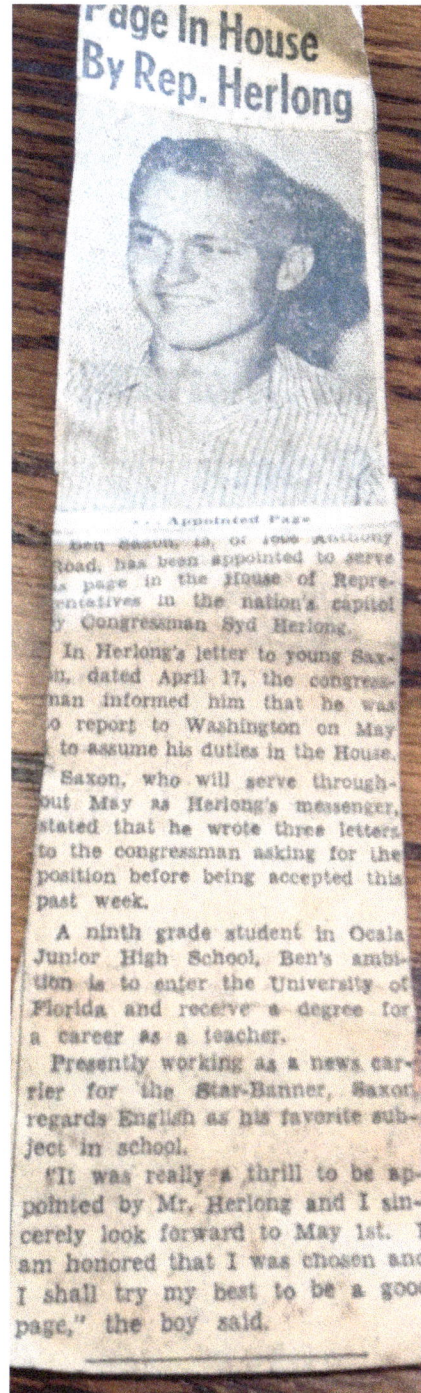

The congressman got letters from many applicants, but he told Ben that he was impressed with his letter because he had the grades and the skills needed to excel. In addition to good grades, Pages were required to be able to read quickly and accurately, write well, and get along with people well enough to interpret the moods of the representatives and senators.

The more attention Ben received, the more resentful his prominent foster family became. The mother of the house was not at all happy that Ben was getting this great opportunity while her son, who was his same age, was not. On the other hand, Mrs. Williams, the lady from welfare, was extremely proud that one of her fosters had been chosen as a Capitol Page. Mrs. Williams borrowed the money that Ben needed for the train trip to Washington, D.C., and she solicited a men's clothing store in Ocala to donate a shirt and dark pants, a coat and some ties, so that Ben would be dressed properly when he arrived. The Pages got paid about $375 per month and Ben was required to pay back the money borrowed for train fare as well as pay for his food. Lodging was provided for the Pages at an apartment house and Ben's room-mate was a Page from Louisiana.

When he arrived in Washington, D.C., Ben went straight to Congressman Herlong's office and his secretary, Mrs. Driesbach, told him where he would be staying. He met his room-mate and then went right to sleep. He was supposed to start on Saturday morning, but overslept and started on Monday. The boys registered for the Capitol Page School on the top floor of the Library of Congress and attended school daily from 5:30 to 7:30 a.m., taking regular subjects. After a 30-minute break, they had to be at work, distributing print-outs of the daily Congressional Record to the various congressmen and running errands until late in the day, when they would return to their lodgings, do their homework, and usually fall into bed exhausted.

"We would get the Congressional Records in stacks from the government printing office, written reports of what transpired in Congress the day before, and we would deliver them and put them in notebooks for each Congressman." When they were finished disseminating the Congressional Records, the Pages would head straight for the back of the House of Representatives waiting for errands to be run for Congressmen, taking the underground passageway and then returning to wait for direction from the head Page. The Head Page was in charge and he would tell them to wait on the benches in the back of the chambers of the House of Representatives until they were required to run an errand. In the cloak room of the House of Representatives there was a small snack shop area where the Pages and the Congressmen could pick up a quick bite to eat before going back to work. There were about ten or twelve Pages on each side, Democratic and Republican. Congressman Herlong was a Democrat.

For the first time in his life, Ben was just like everybody else – not the poor kid, or the foster kid, but simply another Capitol Page running errands and working for his country. In Washington, D.C., nobody knew anything about Ben's personal situation. It felt good to be accepted for his abilities, and people respected the young Pages because each of them had qualified for their position through earning top grades and exhibiting good character. But inside Ben, there still lurked some innate defensiveness and fear of authority. Sometimes he felt like he was in the disguise of a "normal person." The thoughts that ran through his head and the actions he took daily were often in conflict with one another, but despite the temptation to rebel at times, Ben managed to keep his mouth shut and do what he was supposed to do. He did his duties so well that the Congressman asked him to stay longer than the normal one-month assignment. Remaining in Washington, D.C. for nearly eight weeks, Ben attended the Capitol Page School at the Library of Congress until June, and had the opportunity to be shown around Washington, D.C. by Congressman Herlong's secretary and her family. "Mrs. Driesbach was as nice as she could be," recalls Ben. "She went out of her way to make sure I saw some of the historic places in the Capitol."

Working ten to twelve hours or more a day, the Pages had little leisure time, but they were basically on their own as far as how they spent their time off. At 15, Ben sometimes joined the other boys at an Italian restaurant near their apartments, where they ordered pizza and Chianti for dinner. One stand-out memory of his time as a Page in Washington, D.C. was when Ben splurged and asked a cute girl to go to the movies with him. "We saw the movie, Spartacus," he recalls, "and I thought it was the greatest thing in the world to be treated like a human being; to be on my own and taking a girl to the movies."

During his time as a Capitol Page, Ben had the privilege of witnessing history in the making on a daily basis, but one particular day stands out. It was the day he was in the same room with President John F. Kennedy and first lady, Jackie Kennedy, as the president spoke to Congress and the nation at the joint session of Congress on May 25, 1961. The President said, "I believe that this Nation should commit itself to achieving the goal, before this decade is out, of landing a man on the Moon and returning him safely to Earth." The President's and the Nation's goal was achieved by the National Aeronautic and Space Administration (NASA) on

July 20, 1969 with the first manned lunar landing.

"I had the privilege of waiting on both Senators and Representatives and seeing people I never thought I would come into contact with," says Ben, adding that both the President and Jackie Kennedy greeted the congressmen in a friendly manner, going to several and shaking hands. Although Ben wasn't close enough to shake hands with the President or First Lady, as a Capitol Page right there in the House Chambers, he was closer to them and to history than most citizens ever get to be.

Ben's time as a Page in Washington, D.C. gave him a broader vision of the world and cemented his lifelong passion for history. He learned that he could definitely survive on his own; that he could live just as well in the city as he could in the country; that living on a schedule was important, and that people will respect people who respect them. "I also learned that I wasn't as stupid as people made me out to be. I knew I could do whatever it took, but I knew one other thing that I couldn't control. I knew that when this trip was over, I had to go back to my mother and Travis – back to the reality of my life."

Chapter five

The Reality

In June 1961, Ben's time in Washington D.C. came to an end. He remembers the sad ride back to Ocala on the train headed for the shack where his mother and her husband, Travis, lived. He couldn't call it home because he knew he was not wanted there. The one-armed man his mother had married had a grudge against the whole world and a powerfully controlling attitude toward Ben's mother that excluded her children completely. To him, Ben was nothing but a distraction for the woman who was supposed to spend her time waiting only on Travis. Christine spent her days working in the garden and raising goats and pigs, but her main job was taking care of Travis. "Bring me a beer, Christine!" he'd holler when he got out of bed in the morning, and another hard day would begin.

In the meantime, Congressman Herlong, being fully aware that the boy was enduring an untenable situation at the home of his mother and her violent husband, had been actively working behind the scenes to get Ben placed at Rodeheaver Boys Ranch in Palatka, Florida. Founded in 1950 by Evangelist Homer Rodeheaver to take in homeless boys, the Ranch had acquired an unfortunate reputation for taking in juvenile delinquents. Whether or not this reputation was justified, Congressman Herlong had a hard time convincing the Ranch and the courts to place young Ben at the rough and tumble place, with his exemplary reputation and grades good enough to take him to Washington, D.C. Finally, when Herlong convinced the powers that be that Ben had no place else to go, and he was assigned to the Ranch, the boy had no one to take him to Palatka. Once again, Ms. Williams from welfare stepped in and got him a ride to the Ranch.

While he was used to being the smallest boy in class, and was grateful not to quickly outgrow the only clothes he had to his name, Ben was beginning to get taller by the time he arrived at the Ranch. The first thing Ranch Director Skipper Pierce did was send Ben into town with Ranch counselor, Ed Hedstrom, to use some of his (Ben's) hard-earned money for clothing. When you have owned almost nothing all your life, every possession takes on primary importance and, for Ben, the money he had earned and saved as a Capitol Page was his and his alone. This included eight Silver Dollars that he had acquired while in Washington, D.C. When Skipper Pierce told Ben to give him his money, including the Silver Dollars, it was a hard reality that he had no choice. Brooking no argument, Pierce assured Ben that he would take care of his money for him, including the Silver Dollars, but Ben didn't trust him and hid one of the shiny coins back. He never saw the other Silver Dollars again, but has kept the one and still resents the seven he lost. But even more than holding on to possessions and remembering those that have been lost, Ben holds on to memories – both good and bad.

Among his many memories of the Boys Ranch, there is one in particular that still haunts Ben, and that is the day Skip Pierce and Ed Hedstrom took him to Ocala to get the Judge to sign off on the Ranch's custody of Ben. Driving back to the Ranch, Skip and Ed were carrying on a conversation in the front seat while the "new boy" sat quietly in the back seat. "Yes, we've got some smart boys at the Ranch now who may go far," Skip confided to Ed, naming several boys that Ben had met during the past couple of days. Then, as an afterthought, Skip added, "Oh yes, and that one in the back, too."

Ben, on hearing Skip's off-handed remark, scrunched himself even further into the corner of the backseat. He knew that Pierce had simply made that statement because he'd suddenly remembered that Ben, the new boy in the backseat, was overhearing their conversation. For a boy who was used to feeling alone and unwanted, it was just one more confirmation that nobody really thought he would amount to anything. Even having gone to Washington, D.C. as a Capitol Page was not enough to convince anyone that he was a cut above, but Ben sat there in the backseat, fuming and plotting. "I will go further than any of those other boys," he thought to himself. "I will make something of myself no matter what!"

And, while he attempted to get adjusted to being in another new place, surrounded by more new faces, Ben still had one more obligation connected with his time as a Page. He was expected to write thank you letters to Congressman Herlong and the other officials with whom he had associated during his time in Washington, D.C. "I didn't know any better," recalls Ben. "I took notebook paper and tore it in half and wrote thank you notes like that."

Meanwhile, now living in Westbury Cottage in a room with three other boys about his age, Ben was confronted with being the new boy and being challenged by his room-mates on several levels. "What grade you in?" asked one. "I think

I'm in 10th," Ben replied. "I missed a lot of 9th grade but I'm pretty sure I'm ready for 10th." That statement got a bunch of sarcastic looks and comments. Most of the boys at Rodeheaver Boys Ranch back in those days (and still today) were a grade or two behind their age-group due to facing similar challenges that Ben had faced in his young life. But while most of them had accepted their fate and were simply trying to somehow get by, get grown and get away from there, Ben had definite goals. He was going to get top grades in high school and go on to graduate from college. He was going to be a veterinarian, if possible, because he loved animals. Whatever the future held for him, it involved getting ahead and achieving success.

No one at the Ranch thought Ben was ready for 10th grade work, but he insisted he was, so they let him register for 10th grade at Palatka High School, fully expecting him to be put back in 9th the first semester. Ben proved everyone wrong. "Put me in a classroom and tell me I can't do something and watch me do it," says Ben. "I was not going to fail." He made great grades and even was on the honor roll. He did not want to repeat any grades.

That same stubborn tenacity was in the heart and soul of all the Saxon kids, regardless of what hard knocks life held for them.

Jean had found her beloved Harry Acree at a truck stop in Ocala and, in turn, Harry had adopted her three-year old son Bruce and welcomed Emmett as a brother-in-law and friend, but times were tough. Even with Jean and Harry both working, and Emmett taking care of little Bruce, money was tight. Then their first daughter, Dianna Lynn (Sissy), was born and they were thrilled to have the beautiful little baby, but now their money had to stretch even further.

Ben was at Rodeheaver Boys Ranch during those years and Jean would have done anything to get him in her legal custody and take care of him herself, but Ben saw the way things were and didn't want to be a burden on his sister and her little family. After all those years of sitting by the wall at the Mercy Home and pretending the rocks were her house and car and family, Jean finally did have a real family of her own. Ben wasn't about to intrude on that. Oh, but did he ever look forward to those weekends when Jean called ahead to the Ranch and came and picked him up on Saturday morning to spend the night in Ocala and didn't bring him back until Sunday afternoon – the later, the better!

While he would have preferred to be with his sister and her family all the time, Ben was realistic. He was doing well at Palatka High School and he had responsibilities at the Ranch that he could not ignore, both to himself and to the animals. Over the years, his love for animals had become stronger than anything but his love for family. "I was a loner," Ben explains. "People didn't like me, but animals did. They became my best friends."

Ben and a younger boy, Gordon Philbrick, took care of raising the rabbits at the Ranch and enjoyed grooming and riding the horses. After he saw Ben's devotion to animals and how seriously he took the responsibility of caring for them properly, Skipper Pierce put Ben in charge of the horses and horse-back riding. Already misunderstood by the other boys and considered way too ambitious for his own good, that made Ben even more unpopular.

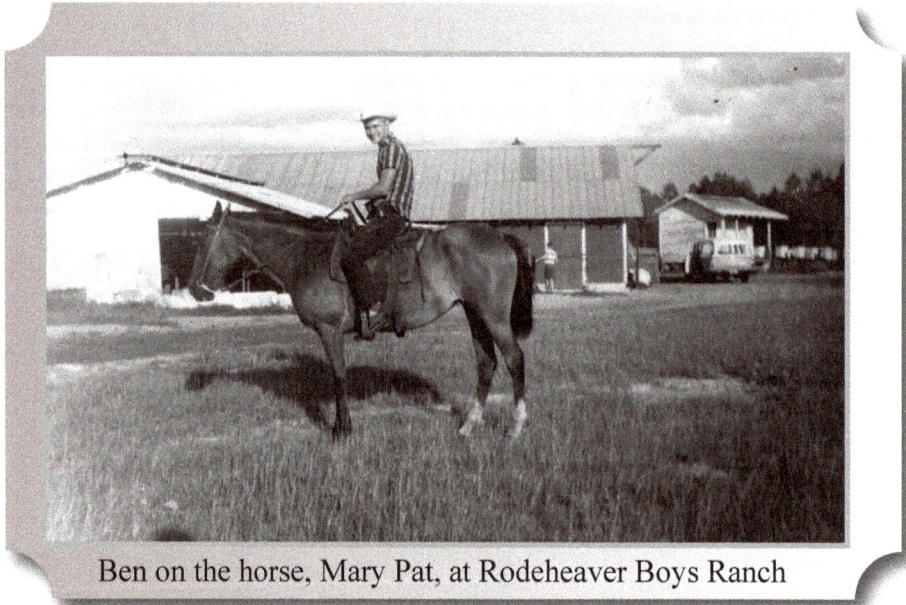

Ben on the horse, Mary Pat, at Rodeheaver Boys Ranch

There were also chickens being raised at the Ranch – many, many chickens - and Ben helped with the chickens, too, but the animal he loved the most was a dog named Dusty.

Dusty had been given to Ben by the grandmother of a friend in Ocala just before he was accepted at the Ranch, and Ben had insisted the dog accompany him when he was taken there. Dusty and Ben were inseparable. Dusty met Ben at the bus every day after school and slept on the front porch of Westbury Cottage. When Ben went horse-back riding, Dusty ran right along beside him. One day, about a year after he arrived at the Ranch, Ben got off the bus and Dusty wasn't there to greet him. Skipper Pierce broke the news to him that Dusty had been bitten by a rattlesnake. They waited until the next day to take him to the vet in town, but he was too far gone. The poison had gone to his heart and Dusty had died at the vet's office so Ben was told. Ben's heart was broken. Dusty was the closest thing to family that Ben had at the Ranch and he missed him fiercely.

In 1963, the summer before Ben went into his senior year in high school, the Mercer Price family of Daytona took him in. They were very wealthy and were supposed to see that Ben would be able to attend college. Unfortunately, Mercer liked his alcohol and did not keep his promises to the Ranch or the boy. Living with them was not pleasant since most of the time because either Mr. Price or his wife was drunk and Ben had to help take care of them. They always went out of their way to make Ben feel guilty because he was being taken in by them. Ben attended Seabreeze Senior High School in Daytona Beach and worked at Publix and life was basically alright until one day in early March of 1964 when Ben and a friend from the Ranch set out to take their SAT's. Ben let the friend drive the family car and they got into an accident. The boy was driving too fast and went off a bridge in Bunnell, Florida, totaling the car. Ben took the blame, saying that he had been the one driving, and the family kicked him out.

Determined to finish out his senior year at Seabreeze High School, Ben turned to his sister, Jean, and asked her to sign the legal custody papers for him, as the state required that anyone under 21 years of age had to have a legal guardian. Jean didn't hesitate, of course, even knowing that Ben was planning to be on his own. She and Harry could barely take care of their family at that point, but she promised Ben they'd help him in any way they could. Ben then proceeded to increase his hours at Publix Supermarket, earning enough money to pay rent for a one room apartment and buy his food.

From March 1964 on, he supported himself and attended high school, graduating from Seabreeze High School with good grades, an NDEA (National Defense Education Act) Grant and various smaller scholarships to attend college. He did not know much about colleges so he spoke with the guidance counselor at Seabreeze who listed several. He applied to only one,

Ben, High School

was interviewed and was immediately accepted at Florida Southern College,

45

a private Methodist college in Lakeland, Florida. He would eventually attend Florida Southern College, later transferring to the University of Florida for his Masters. But even with all of those hard-earned benefits, he still didn't have quite enough money to go to college right away. He stayed out of school for one semester and worked in a 7-Eleven Store to earn some living money and school money. He was completely on his own now.

The year after Ben graduated from high school, Jean and Harry took their family to Harry's hometown of Van, West Virginia. Harry had been a coal miner for years and was going back to coal mining because the money was better. At first, Jean and Harry and the children stayed with Harry's parents, Hazel and Juanita Acree, who welcomed them warmly. Jean and Juanita hit it off right away, getting along more like mother and daughter than in-laws. In fact, later in life, when Juanita moved in with Jean and Harry after Hazel passed away, people often mistook her for Jean's mother. Harry would just laugh and say, "No, she's *my* mother, not hers!"

"Juanita was a good woman," says Jean, laughing at the memory of her beloved mother-in-law. "Everybody liked her and she liked everybody. She was so friendly that if a tree was in front of her, she'd talk to it."

At first, Emmett went to West Virginia with the Acrees, but Jean did not want him to end up in the coal mines. He stayed with them a while and later moved to Nettleton, Mississippi, where he met and married Helen Hendrix. That was when Emmett began driving a truck for a living, going cross-country and making a life of his own as a family man, a Mason and a man of God.

Emmett Saxon, Jr.

Ironically, their little lost sister, Clyde Dean (now Emmaline/Emily) was in middle school in Vicksburg, Mississippi when her oldest brother Emmett moved to Nettleton and her other brother, Ben, graduated from Seabreeze High School in Daytona Beach. In 1966, when her big sister, Jean, was giving birth to her second daughter, Stacy, in West Virginia, Emmaline was graduating from H. V. Cooper High School in Vicksburg and planning to marry her high school sweetheart, Roger Mullings, in January of 1967.

Emmaline Scoggins, 1966

Roger Mullings, 1964

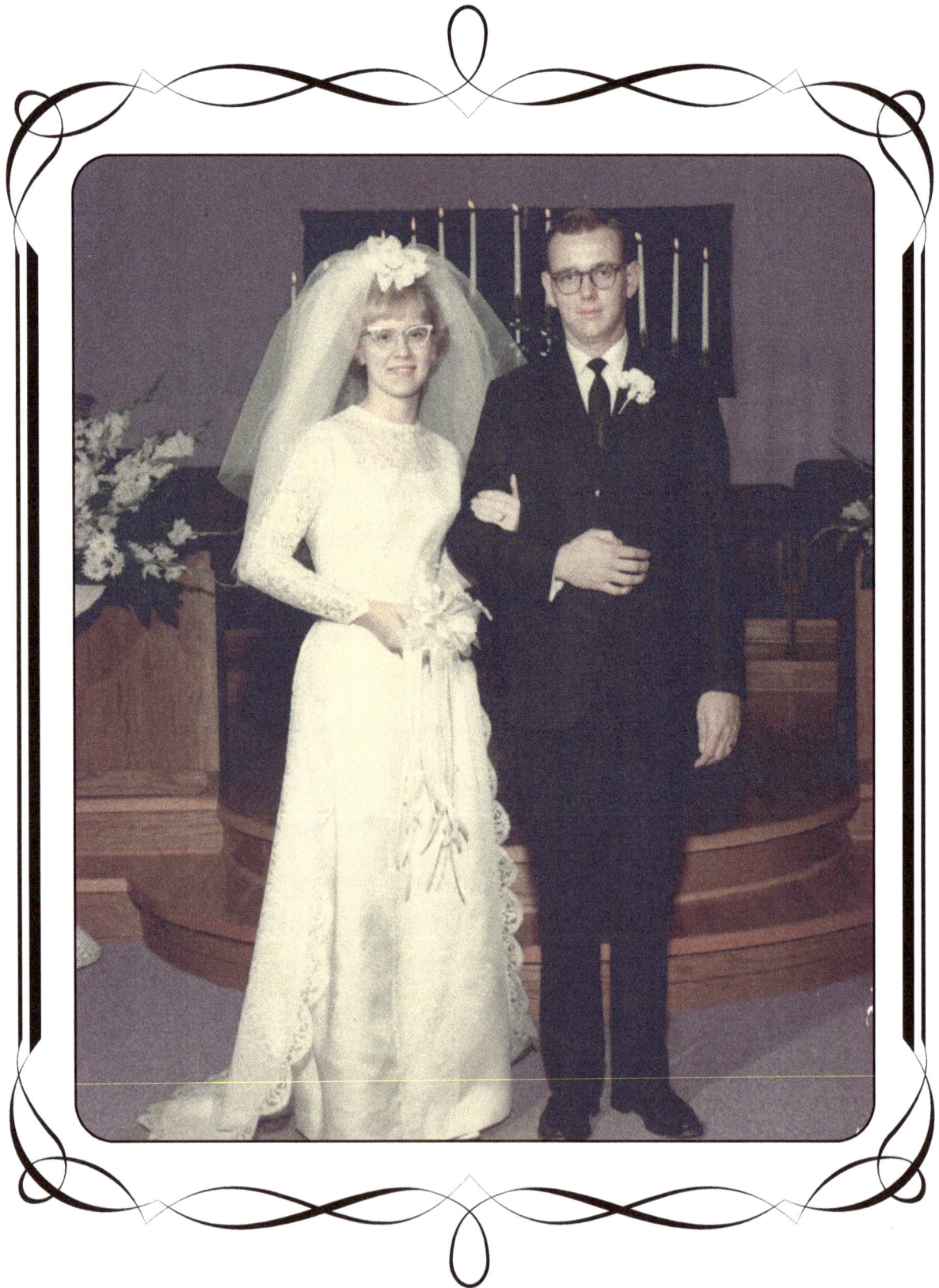

Emmaline and Roger Mullings
January 28, 1967

And, while she was beginning her life with Roger, one of Emmaline's siblings, unbeknownst to her, was already searching for her. Ben remembered being there when his baby sister was born. He often talked about her to Jean and Emmett, and their mother, who had for some reason nicknamed the baby girl "Ricky," was haunted by a memory that she talked about often. When she had gone to the adoption agency to sign away her parental rights, Emmaline had been told that Christine was her mother. At age 5, having been courted regularly for months by her adoptive parents, Virgil and Cecile Scoggins, Emmaline had looked her mother up and down and, pointing at Cecile Scoggins, said, "You're not my mother. She is."

Over the years, Christine begged Ben to find his baby sister, Clyde Dean (Emily/Emmaline), and also to locate Little Debbie (Paula), the other daughter that Christine had given up at birth. As with everything else, Ben took that challenge seriously and had already begun sending out inquiries and following up on leads by the time he graduated.

After graduation, Ben did some traveling. He went to Greensboro, North Carolina to live with a friend. He stayed and worked at Big Bear Supermarket for several months. Later, after he started college, he often took trips to Danville, Virginia … to visit with Hill's grandparents and then to visit his brother, Emmett, in Mississippi, and Jean and her family in Van, West Virginia, but something always drew him back to Florida, where his mother still lived, and where his roots remained strong. Roots and branches … no matter how spread out and diverse they were … Ben was determined to find out about his Saxon heritage and to bring honor to the name. The only way he could do that was to bring the family back together. If they chose not to meet with him when he found them that was their choice. Time frequently drives wedges within families.

Who's who in teachers

OCALA — Six teachers from Marion County and three from Citrus County have been honored by their students, who nominated them for inclusion in "Who's Who Among America's Teachers."

Kathleen Peironnet Cantrell and Ben. L. Saxon of Fort King Middle School; Steven George Northsea of Dunnellon High School; Deborrah Chapin Noxon of Lake Weir Middle School; Linda Nadine Parker of Lake Weir High School; and Randy Mark Swartz of Ocala Christian Academy were nominated from Marion County.

Bonnie Lynn Ignico and Eugene Hyer Trescott Jr. of Citrus High School and George Sewell Bacon of Crystal River High School were nominated from Citrus County.

The teachers were among 24,500 nationwide nominated by former students, all of whom themselves are currently listed in "Who's Who Among American High School Students" or "The National Dean's List," publications that recognize outstanding high school and college students.

The students were asked to nominate teachers who had made a difference in their lives.

Chapter Six

Hard Knocks

Jean and Harry and family were still living in Ocala in December of 1965 when Ben came back from his travels and spent Christmas with them. By then, he and some friends were living in an apartment in Daytona Beach. He was working at the 7-Eleven Store and had bought a 1952 Ford (blue and white, and he thought, pretty classy!). Although he was no closer to having enough money to pursue his real goal of being a veterinarian, Ben knew he had to go on and get started with his college education. He called Florida Southern College in Lakeland to make sure his scholarship was still available and it was. In January of 1965, Ben started at Florida Southern. Since it was a private Methodist College and he was getting a full scholarship which included living on campus, he let Harry drive his car back to Ocala and keep it there for him. While taking classes, at various times he worked at Publix as a bag boy and Winn-Dixie in produce, and in the automotive department at Sears. It was at Sears that he met Kathy, his future wife.

During his second semester at Florida Southern, he took the bus to Ocala and drove his car back, parking it off campus, and he eventually traded it for a 1959 Ford Fairlane, which was not as conspicuous – easier to conceal off campus.

For the last three years at Florida Southern College, Ben lived in the Phi Sigma Kappa Fraternity House, where he acted as a Big Brother to two pledges. His fraternity brothers were from all over the United States. It was a fairly small fraternity – fifteen to twenty members. Ben was also in ROTC in college, but was not called up until 1971. By then, he had already gotten married, had a job teaching, and his wife was expecting a baby. He was drafted by the Army anyway, but was turned down because of suspected contact with a TB patient and because of the pins that were in his leg due to an accident at the Ranch. The suspected TB patient was Pop (his grandfather) but later they found out it wasn't TB.

In addition to being rushed for a Fraternity and being part of ROTC, Ben was also inducted as a founding member into Theta Chi Beta, an Honorary Religious

Fraternity first established as an independent honor society at Syracuse University in 1915. Those who are chosen for Theta Chi Beta Membership are the said to be the embodiment of potential and promise of future distinction in their life's work, and because their professional pursuits reflect an exemplary regard for, and sensitivity to, the study of religion and the religious life itself.

Ben's double major of history with political science and education, with a minor in religion, kept him busy, along with his other activities on and off campus. Ben loved college, and enjoyed every aspect of college life, both working hard and playing hard. His first semester on-campus job working at the administration office helped him buy clothing and books, so that, going forward, he felt that he fit in and was accepted by the other students as a typical classmate, no longer bearing the stigma he had always felt as a foster kid.

Dr. Akerman, who taught political science, was one of Ben's favorite professors at college. He was tough, but a good teacher and Ben found his class enjoyable. Professor Albert was the history professor and Ben found history easy because he was good at remembering dates and the subject fascinated him, but always, in the back of his mind, Ben dreamed of becoming a veterinarian. He took zoology and botany and never gave up completely, but discovered that in order to have his four years of college paid for, he had to choose a four-year goal, and so he chose education. As a result of that choice, for four years of college education, Ben ended up paying a grand total of $300.00, and that only because he interned without pay at Lakeland Junior High School. He graduated on December 15th, 1968 and started teaching on January 10, 1969 at Howard High School in Ocala. Bob Jones, one of his former principals, gave him the job. As soon as he had his first paycheck, Ben moved into an apartment, leaving his mother's house, where (despite protests from Travis) he had temporarily stayed right after graduation because he had no money and no place to go.

Coming in to Howard High School in January, Ben soon found out he was facing quite a few challenges. He was there to replace the previous teacher, who had left abruptly. When he walked into the classroom for the first time, one of the larger 8th graders warned him, "We drove off Miss McClusky. We'll drive you off, too!"

It was a predominantly black student body – grades 7 through 12 - and Ben was tasked with teaching geography and economics to a bunch of rowdy students that did not want to be there. "I had five or six classes of 7th and 8th graders with

30 to 32 kids in each class," recalls Ben. "It was a very interesting year." The windows in the back of his classroom were low to the ground and Ben noticed early on that students crawled out the windows to escape. The teacher next door was a reverend but in no way acted like a man of God. He told Ben "the only thing these kids understand is a strap in your hand." Teachers at Howard regularly had their car tires slashed and one had the top of his convertible cut up. Soon after Ben started teaching at Howard, he was approached by a big senior who towered over him with clenched fists. "You've got my brother in your class..." he said, to which Ben calmly replied, "I'm not mistreating him. I don't mistreat any of my students."

Ben approached teaching as if he were one of his own students, and it worked. He remembered so many years of wishing that his teachers liked him and recognized his abilities and he was determined that he would provide nothing but encouragement to the students in his charge. But first, he had to make his classes interesting enough to keep the kids from sneaking out the back window. He devised a couple of unique methods for teaching geography and economics in such a relevant way that the students actually began staying in class and participating. Addressing the subject of geography, Ben began by describing the present Ocala, Florida location of the students and expanding outward from there. One of the students had a dad who owned a local dry cleaning business with which most of the other students were familiar, so Ben created a virtual dry cleaning business in the classroom in order to teach basic economics. Each day, students would be tasked with answering a question such as how much do you need for the building where your dry cleaner is located, what do you charge to clean various items of clothing, how many employees do you have and what do you pay them per hour ... class discussions were lively and the students' opinions and suggestions were given the respect and attention that Ben had yearned for but never received in his middle school years.

Further, there was the element of fun. Ben knew, from tough experience, that fun and school were not synonymous, and he wanted to change that in his classes. "I made them a promise," he says. "If you will work with me four days a week, on Friday I'll let you play some music and you can show me some dances." Much to the chagrin of the hard-line reverend next door, Ben's students thrived without the need for showing them a strap in hand.

The next year, Ben started teaching at Ft. King Middle School, teaching history and civics to large classes of students from every walk of life. There was one class with 45 students in it, but by then, Ben had learned how to take command of a classroom from day one, and he was also working behind the scenes, taking notes, reading ahead, planning activities and doing his best to anticipate and fill the needs of his many students. Although he never revealed his background to anyone, including his students and fellow teachers, there was an empathy in Ben's teaching style that the students recognized and responded to. They trusted Mr. Saxon and he never let them down. And, besides, his class was fun!

For the first years at Fort King Middle School, where he was destined to teach until he retired in 2008, there was no air conditioning. August and September in Ocala, Florida are hot!! One day, early in the fall, Ben wiped the perspiration off of his forehead, looked around his sweltering classroom and saw that his students were so distracted by the heat that no one could concentrate, so he decided it was time for a fun break! He told his class to close their books, grab a piece of notebook paper and wad it up into a ball. Then, with their teacher in the lead, Ben's class snuck into the hallway and opened the door of the classroom across the hall and at- tacked with a barrage of crumpled up paper balls. Needless to say, the teacher across the hall (who was a friend of Ben's from high school) retaliated soon thereafter, with her students showering Ben's class with paper balls. Although the temperature remained warm, the ensuing paper ball battles definitely cooled things down and allowed the students to return to some semblance of concentration on class subjects. In Mr. Saxon's class, you could expect the unexpected!

By 1971, Ben's life was going along pretty much in the direction he had always hoped it would. He was a teacher, a married man and a homeowner. Kathy was pregnant with their first child, Meredith, who was born on January 24, 1972. Fatherhood fit Ben well and that was a good thing, because there were approximately 150 middle school children who looked up to him as a trusted advisor as well as their mentor and teacher, and there were a few to whom he was almost considered a surrogate father. A letter from one of his former students illustrates the extraordinary relationship that evolved between teacher and student as Ben's career advanced from year to year:

The Outsider that Cared

Mr. Saxon was my seventh and eighth grade history teacher. He had no idea who I was or what my home life was like. All he knew was that I was having a hard time in school my seventh grade year.

Mr. Saxon took me under his wing and nurtured my hurt feelings and confused mind. He helped me in so many ways that I cannot even count them all. He worked with my mother to get to the source of my problems, and, once found, helped me deal with them.

I was a stranger to him at the beginning of the year, but he showed so much love and compassion toward me that I trusted him more than anyone else except my mother.

He helped me deal with my mom's ex-boyfriend, who was causing a lot of trouble and stress. He beat my mom and was always bothering the entire family.

He [Mr. Saxon] helped me get my grades back up, and keep them up. He gave me a reason to want good grades, to make him proud of me.

He did all this by showing me that there were other people in the world that loved me, not just my mom. Since my dad left when I was six months old, and I hardly saw him, I figured that my close relatives were the only ones that would or could ever love me. He showed me otherwise. I love him just as I would if he were my biological father.

In the meantime, Jean and Harry had been in West Virginia for nearly three years by the time Ben began teaching school. Jean had given birth to their second baby girl, Stacy. In the winter of 1969 they decided to move their little family of four back to Ocala, because coal mining didn't pay the bills and the job at the truck stop in Ocala was still available for Harry. So, during the summer after his graduation from college, Ben had driven to West Virginia and helped Jean and family move back to Ocala.

With the encouragement of her brothers and her husband, Jean finally began to pursue her dream of being a hair stylist. She signed up for cosmetology classes at the College of Central Florida. By the early 70's, Jean had earned her cosmetology degree and was working as a beautician, but now that her dream was reality, being a hair stylist turned out not to be as lucrative or as enjoyable as she had envisioned it to be. Jean had always been a loner and now she was in a daily environment where she was surrounded by the buzz of women laughing and talking all around her (most of the talk involving gossip on subjects that she preferred not to discuss in public). "I just kept to myself and did my job," she recalls. "I never added much to the conversation in the beauty salon."

When a job in the Cosmetology Department of Walgreen's came open in 1975, Jean took it. Fortunately, she had grown up working hard because the job at Walgreen's was a demanding one with long hours that often kept her at the store during holidays and school breaks. That job lasted nine years and her supervisor became so dependent on Jean that she was called on to do just about everything and be at the store just about every day. Whenever she threatened to look for another job, her supervisor begged her to stay and offered to raise her pay, but she wanted more than a raise in salary – she wanted some sort of security – the kind of security a pension and benefits would give her. When Jean expressed to Ben that she was really getting burned out at Walgreen's, he started keeping an eye out for a better job for her with the Marion County Public School System.

"A friend, Sandy Ayers, worked with ARC for the school district," recalls Ben, "and when Sandy told me she was looking for a teacher for developmentally disabled adults, I knew Jean was perfect for the job. There were a bunch of job applicants, but when Jean took all the qualifying tests and passed them with flying colors, Sandy hired her immediately. They worked together for years. Jean had just the sensitivity needed for the job. She was great at it!"

Back in the early 1970's, after Ben was married and teaching school and Jean and Harry had moved back to Ocala with their family, Emmett worked for a while with Harry at the truck stop, but he was lonely. Just like his brother and sister, he had always yearned for a family of his own. He married a girl he met at the truck stop and that marriage lasted about two weeks. It seemed that Emmett just couldn't find his niche in life.

"He was so quiet and withdrawn that he was overlooked," recalls Ben, "We had both been taught that you open your mouth, you get a fist stuck in it."

The only time that Emmett seemed to open up and have fun was when he was at the truck stop with the Acree brothers, Harry and Larry. "Emmett and Larry used to play pranks on Harry," recalls Jean. "Just as he was about to finish work, one of them would tell him he needed to take the wrecker to South Florida. Harry would call to tell me he wouldn't be home for dinner and I'd hear them laughing in the background. The three of them together were something!"

Ben didn't see much of Emmett in those days, as their lives were on different paths, but one day, Emmett surprised his younger brother by coming to him for advice. "I have a friend who has a sister up in Nettleton, Mississippi that is looking for somebody to be friends with," he told Ben. "I'd like to go meet her and if we get along, I may marry her." Ben knew how lonely his brother was and how much he wanted a family. He also knew Emmett well enough to know that he'd do what he wanted to anyway, so he backed him up with encouragement and told him to go for it. As it turned out, Helen, the woman in Nettleton, Mississippi already had one daughter when Emmett married her. They later had Emmett's only daughter, Loressa, but Emmett treated both girls like they were his own. Emmett got a job with Malone & Hyde as a transcontinental truck driver and, for the next thirty years, drove trucks cross-country. Having never had an accident in his entire truck-driving career, Emmett received several awards and safe-driving pins over the years from his company. He also became a Mason and was extremely active in a non-denominational Christian church in his community. While life wasn't perfect for Emmett Saxon – and he continued to suffer residual problems both physically and emotionally from his early childhood - he worked hard, became a productive citizen and took good care of his family.

As her long lost siblings made their livings and raised their families on the East Coast of the United States, Emily and her husband Roger traveled to Panama in the Canal Zone, living there for three years. It was there that Emily gave birth to their first son, Glenn, in 1968. In 1971, while Jean was getting her cosmetology degree and Ben was teaching school and Emmett was beginning his career as a long-distance truck driver, Emily was giving birth to her second son, Michael, in Pensacola, Florida, where her husband Roger Mullings was an instructor at the Naval Base. The Mullings next tour of duty was in Guam, where their third son Scott, was born in 1977, and from Guam, the family moved to Hawaii. There, Roger reinlisted in the Navy on a boat adjacent to the Arizona Memorial.

Roger reinlists

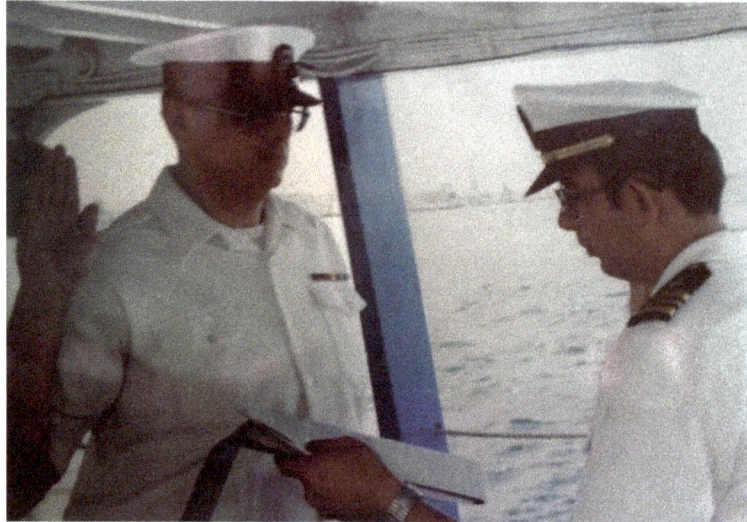

"Hawaii was a favorite place to live," recalls Emily. "The boys were active in school, soccer and Boy Scouts."

In those years when it was just the three of them, Ben, Emmett and Jean thought often of their lost sister, Clyde Dean (Emily). They also wondered about their half-sister, Debbie, whom their mother had told them was given into foster care at the hospital in Birmingham where she was born and legally adopted at age two. They were later to learn, thanks to extensive searching and, finally, the services of a private investigator, that their youngest sister, Debbie (now named Paula), had been adopted by the Woodall family of Tuskegee, Alabama, on February 13, 1952, at five months old.

Four years younger than Emily, Paula knew from the beginning that she was adopted, but had never been told anything about her birth family. She was an adored only child like her sister, Emily, and her mother did not provide her information about her birth. Once, after she reached adulthood, Paula went personally to the adoption agency, having been told that records were sealed and only she could see them. She sat with the files in her hand but was not allowed to make copies and could only attempt to memorize the information. Her mother's name was Christine Juliette Saxon, according to her original birth certificate, and her own name on the same birth certificate simply read "Baby Saxon." She left the agency knowing little more than she knew when she arrived, and with no cooperation (in fact, some resistance) from her adoptive mother, she simply put away her curiosity about her roots for another day. That day was to come in early spring of 1985 when a strong male voice on the phone said, "This is your brother, Ben Saxon."

Christine "Juliette" Saxon Sloan had never been given a middle name, and when she had the opportunity, she had chosen the middle name of Juliette. She lived with her husband, Travis Sloan, in Ocala for many years, always trying to somehow reconcile with her three remaining children. Jean, Ben and Emmett each, in their own way, tried to be kind to their mother despite her history of neglecting them and the total rejection they received from Travis. Christine spent most of her time waiting on Travis, and when she could spare the time, she worked in her garden and raised her goats and pigs. In 1979, Travis decided to move to Warrior, Alabama and Christine moved with him. A few months after their move, Christine was diagnosed with lung cancer, and on November 15, 1980, she passed away at Cooper Green Memorial Hospital in Birmingham, Alabama.

Jean, Ben and Emmett were there in her last hours. Each of them stood by her bed and reflected on the rare happy memories they had of their mother and, as for Ben, often called "cotton-top" as a boy because of his white-blonde hair, a harsh memory flashed through his mind … a mind-picture of four little kids in the cotton fields, the youngest a toddler still in diapers, dragging burlap bags down row after row, picking cotton until their fingers bled so that their mother and father could buy cigarettes.

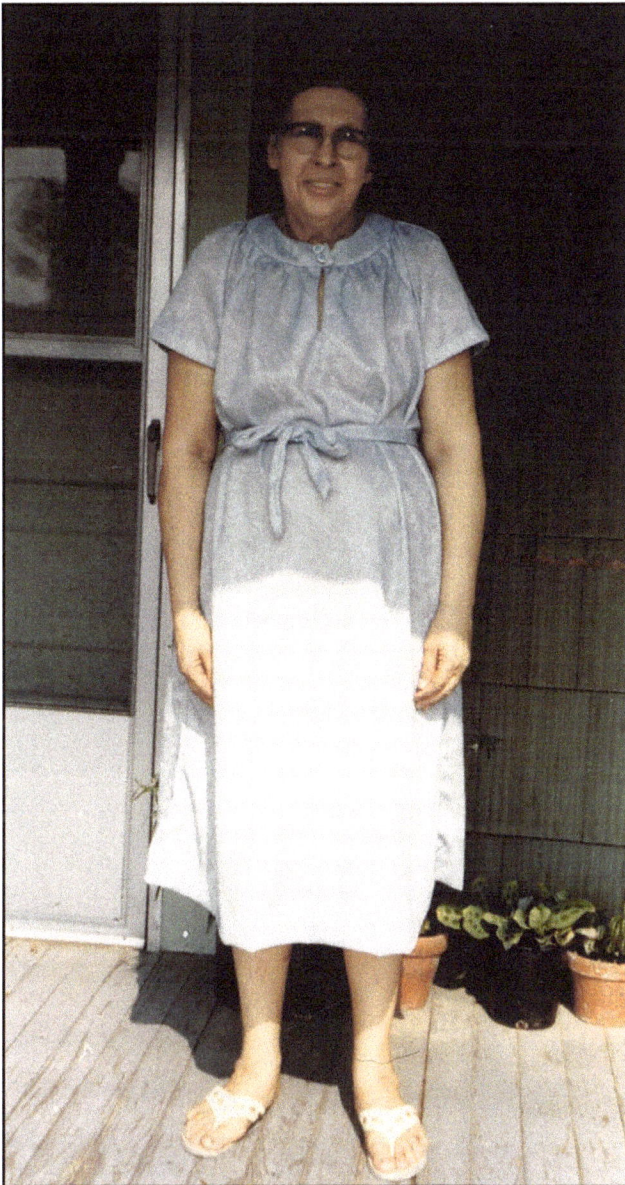

**Christine "Juliette" Saxon Sloan
in later years.**

Sadly remembering more hard times than good times with their mother, the three siblings buried her in Warrior Memorial Cemetery and returned to their families and their lives. She had left them many times in the past, but this time they missed her more deeply than ever before – this time, she was gone for good.

Far away in Hawaii, on November 15, 1980, a Navy wife and the mother of three active boys became extremely ill for no apparent reason. "I didn't understand what hit me," says Emily. "There's still no logical explanation for that terrible sick-spell, but I have to believe it had something to do with the death of our mother and the deep sadness of my sister and brothers."

Paula Woodall Manning, Christine's youngest daughter, knew nothing about her mother's death until five years later when she met her siblings for the first time. "I didn't know where my mother's grave was, but about fifteen years ago, I went by myself to Warrior, Alabama and got out of the car and stood by her grave talking to her. I asked her to send me a sign that she knew I was there, as I had not seen her since my birth. Suddenly, two big cow birds swooped down out of the woods and one came so close I had to duck. It could have been her. I still visit her grave and put flowers on it every couple of years."

There was a time in 2014 when Paula knew with absolute certainty that her mother was aware of her comings and goings. It was a time of transition for Paula and she had driven to a nearby town to interview for a

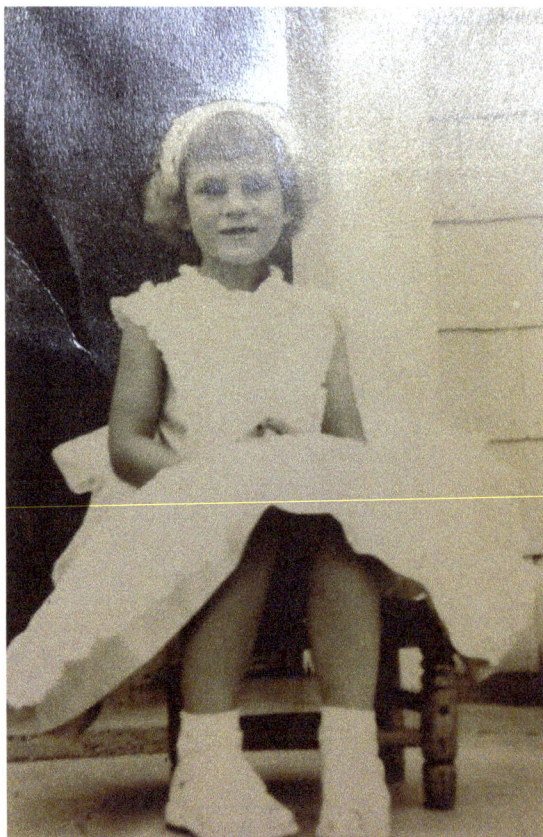

Paula Woodall Manning

nursing job that she very much wanted. Getting there a bit early, she pulled into a MacDonald's across the street to get a coke and say a quick prayer before the interview. As she sat looking out the window, a white truck pulled up right in front of the building where she had the appointment. On the side of the truck were the words "Lil Debbie." Paula was stunned. Her siblings had told her that her mother, Christine, had always referred to her as "little Debbie" when talking about her long lost youngest daughter. "I knew it was a sign from my mother that my prayers were going to be answered and I would get this job," said Paula, "and sure enough, I got it."

Like Paula, Emily had no memories of their mother. She had never met Christine's husband, Travis, or spent any time with her mother after age two, but by the summer of 1989, Emily had heard the stories of Travis and his cruelty. When she went to visit her mother's grave in Warrior, Alabama, she was starkly aware of the differences between the two people buried side by side in that cemetery, and how those differences were physically reflected. Christine's grave was covered with soft green grass and Travis's grave was brown and thorny.

Eerily, all three sisters (each raised in entirely different circumstances) share a strong belief in the existence of spiritual messages from beyond, and each of them has sensed the presence of their mother in their lives, especially since they've known one another. "We were all born to the same mother," says Jean. "She had ESP (Extra Sensory Perception), and so do we. Mother and I used to have the same dreams. My daughter, Stacy, has it, and so did my son, Bruce, but not my daughter, Sissy. I'm not surprised my sisters have it. ESP runs in our mother's side of the family."

Family ... the power of that word is huge. Yes, even though they were separated by years and memories and miles, the Saxons seemed to share a bond of blood that was unbreakable.

Christine
"Juliette"
Saxon

Chapter Seven

Reunion!

Once they were grown, and well before their mother passed away in 1980, Ben, Jean and Emmett began in earnest to search for their baby sister, Clyde Dean. They were determined to eventually find their half-sister as well, but they weren't even sure of her name and with such scant information on her, they pursued the sister they all knew and remembered as a baby. It was their hope that they would find Clyde Dean and reunite her with their mother as well as themselves, but that was not to be. Their search went on for many years, with Jean and Ben writing letter after letter while Emmett asked questions and made phone calls as he drove from town to town.

Among the many letters that were written by Jean in search of her sister Clyde Dean was one on July 8, 1977 to Gateway in Birmingham, Alabama (formerly known as the Mercy Home, where she and Ben and Emmett had been placed as children). Jean received the following response from Mrs. Martha F. Waters, the Director of Family and Child Services at Gateway, on August 15, 1977:

Dear Mrs. Acree:
In response to your letter of July 8, 1977, I have searched our files and have been unable to determine information regarding the adoption placement of your sister Clydene. I have found out that it was not handled by the Children's Aid Society here in Birmingham. That probably means she was placed by the Alabama State Department of Pensions and Security.

You may want to inquire of them though I doubt they can legally release information to you unless your sister Clydene requests information about her family. Their address is Alabama Department of Pensions and Security, Adoptions Division, 5th Floor, Administration Building, 64 North Union Street, Montgomery, Alabama 36104.

I'm sorry we could not be of more help.

Sincerely,
Martha F. Waters, ACS

On August 17, 1977, following receipt of the above letter, Jean wrote a letter "To Whom It May Concern," and mailed it to the Alabama Department of Pensions and Security, Adoptions Division, stating:

> *My brother and I are trying to locate our sister, Clyde Dean Saxon, who was adopted out at the age of 2 years, Birth Date August 26, 1947. My two brothers, Ben Saxon, Emmett Saxon and I, Jeannette Saxon (Acree) where placed in a children's home known as the Mercy Home then, but it has since changed its name to Gateway in Birmingham, Alabama. My sister Clyde Dean was too young to be placed in the home and was adopted out in 1950 or 1951, possibly. The Children's Aid Society in Birmingham, Alabama, did not handle this. We're hoping maybe she knows she's adopted and is trying to find us.*
>
> *Could you possibly be able to help us? Looking forward to hearing from you as soon as possible.*
>
> *Sincerely,*
> *(Jeannette Saxon)*
> *Mrs. Jean Acree*

In the above handwritten letter, she listed her birth date and address, and those of her brothers, and the names of their parents, Emmett Richmond Saxon Sr. and Christine Juliette Saxon.

In a letter dated August 26, 1977, Miss Nell English, Supervisor, Division of Adoption, the State of Alabama Department of Pensions and Security, responded to Jean's letter as follows:

Dear Mrs. Acree,

Your letter of August 17 has been referred to me for reply.

I understand that you and your brothers are trying to locate your sister, who was removed from the family at two years of age and was placed for adoption.

You may be aware that persons who were adopted and who were placed by the Department may return to the Department to ask for information about their placement after they reach adulthood. I am not on the other hand able to give you information about Clydene's whereabouts.

She is aware of her adoption, and it is possible that she may get in touch with us at some time in the future to ask our help in locating you. If she does that, we will be happy to make every effort to find you.

The age of adulthood in Alabama formerly was 21 years. A recent Alabama law sets the age of adulthood at age 19. Clydene, of course, is way over this age so there would be no problem in our sharing information with her when she requests it.

We will not be able to give her identifying information about any family members without the permission of those family members. I am, therefore, filing your letter which gives the names and addresses of your brothers, as well as your name and address. I will keep these in case Clydene does make some request of us to locate you.

In the meantime if either of the three of you should move and wish to give us your new address, we will be glad to have this.

I assure you of our interest in your request, and we will be glad to get in touch with you if Clydene makes inquiry.

Sincerely yours,
(Miss) Nell English, Supervisor

For many years, letters from Ben and Jean went out to churches, newspapers, agencies, individuals ... anyone they thought might have some kind of lead on their sister, Clyde Dean (or Clydene, depending on who was writing who). As their mother aged, she often spoke about her two missing daughters, Clyde Dean (whom she sometimes called Rickie), and the daughter she had given into foster care at the hospital in 1951, their youngest sister, "little Debbie."

"Find them for me, Ben," she'd plead. "Find my girls for me."

After Christine died in 1980, Ben, Jean and Emmett kept hearing her voice in their heads ... "Find my girls, find my girls ... find my Rickie, find my girls." They renewed their efforts. The years were slipping by and none of them were getting any younger, including their two lost sisters. "Having a missing sister was like missing a piece of myself," says Jean. "After all, I carried Clyde Dean on my left hip from the time that little girl was born ... that's why I walk crooked to this day!" Seriously, though, Jean, Emmett and Ben needed the closure of finding their lost sisters. They needed desperately to feel like a real family, as they had never truly experienced that feeling growing up. Ben, especially, attempted to keep his distance from the emotional side of the search, regularly stating that it would be alright with him if his sisters didn't want to be reunited as long as they knew they were wanted; that he was just doing his best to carry out his mother's wishes, but deep inside, Ben was still that sad, angry little boy kicking dirt on the hot Alabama Road and wishing somebody would care about him. All three of the Saxon kids ... now grown up with families of their own, had a sincere desire to know what happened to their sisters and to make them a permanent part of their lives.

In August of 1984, a letter was sent by Ben, listing Jean and Emmett as participants in the letter, to newspapers throughout the Southeastern United States. It read as follows:

Dear ...

As children our family was separated. My sister, brother and myself are attempting to locate two younger sisters who were adopted. I returned from Montgomery, Alabama earlier this month with a little more information and hope that if this information is published in your newspaper it will be seen by our sisters or someone who would notify them of it.

The information we have so far is as follows:

Sister #1 - Name: Clyde Dean Saxon
D.O.B. 08/26/47
Birthplace: Winter Haven, FL
Placed in foster care at the age of 2, adopted
at age 6 in the spring of 1952; name changed
at that time. Living in Pratt City, Alabama at
the time of foster care placement. Adopted
to an Alabama family. In 1976, adoptive
mother contacted Office of Pensions and
Securities in Montgomery to inquire how her
daughter could locate her birth family.

Sister #2 - Name: Rickie (Debbie) Saxon
D.O.B. 08/29/51
Birthplace: Birmingham, ALA
Placed in foster care from hospital.
Called Rickie by her foster parents. All
records, until the time of her adoption, refer
to name Rickie. She was adopted at age 2.
Her name was changed at that time.

We have contacted your newspaper by phone but were told that they could not print a name in the classified ad section without the parties permission. It was suggested that we contact you to see if this letter could be published in the "Letter to the Editor" section.

We would appreciate any means by which you might help us with our search. We would like very much to bring our family back together.

Thank you for your interest and consideration. If you have any questions please contact me and have all inquiries sent to the address below.

Sincerely,
Ben L. Saxon
Emmett Saxon
Jean Saxon Acree
Ocala, FL 32678

The Managing Editor of the Tuscaloosa News, Ellison Clary, responded on August 30, 1984, with basically the same response they received from several of the newspapers that received their letter:

> Dear Mr. Saxon:
>
> Mr. Charles Land passed your letter on to me. It is not of the nature of letter we used in our letters to the Editor column. I recommend that you search for the two younger sisters through government channels. I wish you well in that regard.
>
> Sincerely,
> Ellison Clary

Also, as their extensive search widened, Ben perused publications that had to do with finding missing persons, one of which was *The War Cry* magazine published by the Salvation Army. In answer to his letter of August 20, 1984 to that magazine, Ben received a letter dated September 7, 1984 from (Mrs.) Dorothy Hicks, Supervisor, Missing Persons Services, Salvation Army, Southern Territorial Headquarters, Atlanta, Georgia:

> Dear Mr. Saxon:
> This will acknowledge your August 20 request for assistance in locating your sisters, Clyde Dean Saxon and Rickie (Debbie) Saxon.
>
> Please find enclosed a list of the guidelines which govern Missing Persons Services, on which you will note that we are not permitted to search for individuals where adoption is involved. This is because we work primarily through a number of agencies, and many of them will not release to us any information regarding individuals who have been adopted. Also, Clyde Dean and Debbie would now have not only adopted maiden names but probably married names as well. Without knowing a person's current correct name, to locate her would be next to impossible.
>
> With regard to advertising in <u>The War Cry</u>, we cannot do this because we have no idea how much your sisters now know about their background. Debbie might not even know that her birth name was Saxon or even that they was adopted. Having this advertising might create embarrassing and/or disruptive circumstances for which we could not accept responsibility. Even your sister who was adopted at age six probably would not remember you or other members of her natural family. We are so sorry that we cannot make the search; we can well understand that you long to see your sisters again.

We note that the Office of Pensions and Securities has been in touch with Clyde Dean's adoptive mother. In this case, this office should still have a record of this contact, and perhaps they can assist you in finding your sister's adoptive mother. We do not know whether or not they would be at liberty to help you, but if you have not tried to secure information already through this agency, we would suggest that you write to the following person:

Ms. Ada Kate Morgan, Director
Montgomery County Department of Pensions and Security
P. O. Box 2807
Montgomery, Alabama 36194 (205) 284-3850

We hope that this organization will be able to assist you. We are so sorry that we cannot be of help to you. Perhaps The Salvation Army can assist you at another time.

Please be assured of our interest and desire to be of service to all whenever possible.

May God bless you, Mr. Saxon.

Sincerely yours,
(Mrs.) Dorothy Hicks, Supervisor

Ben and Jean also continued sending letters to churches in the same areas of Alabama where their sisters may have been raised. One of the two churches that responded was First Baptist Church of Jacksonville, Alabama. In a letter dated October 8, 1984, Pastor John Norman wrote:

Dear Mr. Saxon:
I have passed along your letter of inquiry about your two sisters to our church secretary and church clerk who are searching our records for the names you supplied.

Any information we uncover will be forwarded to you. Our prayers and good wishes are with you in your quest to locate these two persons dear to you.

Sincerely yours,
John Norman, Pastor

An October 11, 1984 letter from Pastor Barney Austin at the Oak Bowery Baptist Church in Ohatchee, Alabama was enthusiastic, but still there was nothing new to report:

> *Dear Saxons:*
>
> *I read your letter in one of our services recently and then left the letter on the front for others to read if they felt they could help you in your search. As of this date no one has been able to remember anything that could be of any help in your search. If you should come up with any more information that might help to jog the memories we will be more than happy to pass it along for their consideration.*
>
> *I will keep your letter on file just in case someone should want to read it again. If we can be of any further help or assistance please don't hesitate to advise us. May God Bless you as you seek his will for all your lives.*
>
> *Sincerely,*
>
> *Barney Austin, Pastor*

A man named John Saxon (no relation) in Ragland, Alabama, heard through his church about the search for the two missing Saxon sisters and called Ben. Ben traveled to meet him and also sent him the following very detailed hand-written letter outlining everything that had transpired in their search to date. The letter to John Saxon, below, was written sometime in late October 1984, at a time when Ben and his siblings were beginning to think they had exhausted all avenues, but, being the Saxons they were, had no intention of giving up:

> *Dear John,*
>
> *Well this is going to be quite a feat to tell you all I know so I guess I had better begin. I'll start with myself –*
>
> *Full name – Ben Lee Saxon*
>
> *D.O.B. 12-5-45 Birthplace: Winter haven, Fla.*
>
> *Father: Emmett Richmond Saxon Sr.*
>
> *Mother: Christine Juliette Fleming*
>
> *Paternal Grandfather: Richmond Eli Saxon*
>
> *Paternal Grandmother: Julia Hudspeth*
>
> *Maternal Grandfather: William Hampton Fleming*
>
> *Maternal Grandmother: Emma Pearl Kent*
>
> *At age 3 ½, I was taken to the Mercy Children's Home in Woodlawn, Alabama after my father left us. My sister Jeannette and brother Emmett were also placed at the Mercy Home with me. It was apparently determined*

that our younger sister Clyde Dean was too young to be placed in the Mercy Home so she was placed in foster care.

I lived at the Mercy Home for seven years. I left the Mercy Home at age 11 and was placed in foster care – from the foster home I went to live with my mother and step-father which didn't work out. I was placed in foster care again living with the Morningstar family in Ocala, Fla. It was then that I applied and was appointed to be a page for Congressman Sidney Herlong in the U.S. Congress. I lived in Washington, D.C. and served as his page and received h.s. for my education. When it came time for me to return home, I went to Congressman Herlong and expressed the desire to not return to my mother and stepfather. Congressman Herlong was instrumental in securing a place for me at Rodeheaver Boy's Ranch in Palatka, Fla. I remained there until age 17 when I was again placed in foster care and moved to Daytona Beach, Florida to live with the Mercer Price family. I finished my H.S. Education at Seabreeze High School in Daytona Beach. I received a scholarship to Florida Southern College where I remained for four years. My major was History and Political Science. My minor was Religion and Education. Then I got a teaching job at Howard H. S. In Ocala. I married Kathy E. Perkins in 1969. We have two children ages 12 ½ and 9 ½. I went back to school in 1980 and received a Masters Degree from the University of Florida. I'm now teaching at Ft. King Middle School where I have been for the last 15 years.

Our mother was Southern Baptist, however, I was raised in the Methodist faith. At present we are members of the First Presbyterian Church, Ocala, and our children attend Grace Episcopal Day School.

Our father was in the Merchant Marines (so we were told). After he left us the only thing I know is that he traveled quite a bit and lived in many different places. We finally found him when he was dying at Durham Medical Center in Durham, NC. He apparently spoke of his brother Curtis who, as far as we know, still resides in Tallahassee. The hospital contacted Curt Saxon and he and their sister Clyde Dean traveled to Durham to see him prior to his death (so they said). They said he identified old pictures of his children and called us by name. He died in March 1972 and is buried in Blakely Memorial Cemetery, Blakely, GA in the Saxon family plot.

My Uncle Curt worked at the State Department in Tallahassee after retiring from the railroad. Aunt Clyde Dean married D. T. Norwood and also lives in Tallahassee. Since my father's death they have made no effort to contact us or have anything to do with us.

Our mother remarried Travis Sloan and lived in Ocala for many years. One year before our mother died her husband moved her to Warrier, Ala. A few months later, they discovered she had cancer. She died in Cooper Green Memorial Hospital in Birmingham, Ala. In November 1980. She is buried in Warrior Memorial Cemetery. She was 58 when she died.

We have tried many times over the years to locate our sisters. Our mother gave us bits and pieces of information before she died.

Mrs. Ruth Williams, a case worker in Ocala who worked with me as a child, has called Montgomery and was told there were pictures of us as children, but she was not able to secure any information that we could really sink our teeth into.

Our mother spoke of our two sisters. The information she gave was that Clyde Dean Saxon, the oldest of the two, was born in Winter Haven, Fla. And Debbie Saxon was born in Birmingham, Alabama and they were adopted. She said Clyde Dean was born with a birthmark on her left forearm. I contacted Winter Haven trying to locate a birth certificate but they could not give me any information. They stated her birth certificate would be located in Jacksonville but if she was adopted that it would be sealed. I have not tried to contact Jacksonville.

A few months ago Ruth Williams from family services in Ocala called me to discuss my search. She suggested that we contact the Bureau of Pensions and Securities in Montgomery, Ala.

After Ms. Williams' phone call my wife and I decided to plan our vacation around a trip to Montgomery. We went to Athens, Ga. To work on genealogy, visited two other cities in Georgia and then went to Montgomery.

We went to the Bureau of Pensions and Securities and spoke to Jerry Milner. He could not locate any pictures in our sister's file but he did give us the following information:

Sister #1 – Name: Clyde Dean Saxon
DOB 08/26/47
Birthplace Winter Haven, Fla.
Placed in foster care at age of 2, adopted at age 6 (in the spring of 1952) name changed at that time. Living in Pratt City, Alabama at

the time of foster care placement.

Adopted to an Alabama family. In 1976 Adoptive mother contacted office of Pensions & Securities in Montgomery to inquire how her daughter could find out information concerning her birth family.

Sister #2 – Name: (Debbie) Saxon
DOB 08/29/51
Birthplace: Birmingham, Ala.

Placed in foster care from the hospital (adopted). Called Debbie(?) by her foster parents. (One sister was called Rickie and the other Debbie by our mother.) Mr. Milner indicated that even though our mother apparently intended to name her Debbie, the name never got put on the birth certificate. All records until the time of her adoption refer to the name Debbie. She was formally adopted at age 2. The name was changed at that time.

Mr. Milner indicated that our mother tried very hard to get the entire family back together but that she was not able to do that. She finally signed for the two younger children to be adopted several years after foster care placement.

Since we returned home from our visit to Montgomery and learned that Clyde Dean was not adopted until age 5 and inquiries had been made in 1976, we decided to intensify our efforts to find our sisters.

We feel that if a child was called Clyde Dean for 5 years, even though her name may have been changed, she would probably have recollection of the name Clyde Dean. Therefore, we have sent the attached letter to every major newspaper in Alabama hoping they would publish the information. I have written to Kathy Windel in California in response to a magazine article we read about her locating her own daughter. She is now operating a search organization.

We have contacted a local judge and attorney to see if anything could be done legally. They indicated another state was out of their jurisdiction that we should contact the Alabama legal system. I have written a letter of plea to Alabama Governor George Wallace. I have yet to receive a reply.

I have contacted the War Cry Magazine published by the salvation Army in response to an anonymous postcard we received from Alabama after the publication of our letter in one of the newspapers. No response as yet.

I have also written to Dear Abby hoping she might publish our plea or offer other channels which we might try.

At this point in our search we feel so very close yet so far away, however, each time we check the post office box we find notes, cards, tapes from very special people who wish us well. It's amazing how many people whom you don't even know, are so kind.

Well John I guess that is about it. Anything you can do will be appreciated so much. Thank you for the tape, you sound like quite a character. We also enjoyed the gospel music very much. It sounds as if you have two very fine daughters.

As we discussed, I don't want to just pop up as the long lost brother to my sisters but I would appreciate it if someone could contact them, tell them of our existence and then if they choose to contact us that's fine. I respect their privacy and could live with not knowing them as long as I knew that was their choice.

Thank you again for everything. I'll be in touch.

May God Bless You
Ben Saxon

What Ben didn't tell John Saxon, who was a fundamental Christian and might not understand, was that he and Jean had even gone to the legendary town of Cassadega, Florida where they had consulted with psychics and mediums in search of their sisters. Jean was told very definitely by one fortune teller that her sister was overseas, which is one of the few truths that came out of their visits. Ben, Jean and Emmett had literally used nearly every means available to search for their sisters, but there was still one they hadn't tried.

It was during the week before Thanksgiving, 1984, that Ben read an interesting article in the Ocala Star Newspaper about a long lost relative being found by a local private detective. This was an avenue they had not considered before. Ben took note of the name of the investigative agency, Checkmate Investigation, and called for an appointment right away. The investigator informed Ben that he worked on a contingency basis, keeping track of his time and travel and charging his client when the mission was accomplished - the mission in this case - to find two long-lost sisters! Ben wasn't sure how he was going to pay for it, but he hired the investigator knowing that he'd find a way to pay if success was achieved, just as he had always found a way to do whatever he was determined to do. Within just two months, both Clyde Dean (Emily) and Debbie (Paula) had been found! When Ben was presented with a $600 bill in January 1985, he did what he had to do ... sold one of his most cherished possessions, his classic 1966 burgundy and white Chevy Caprice. "That car was loaded," Ben says. "It had a V-8 engine, a spotless interior, all the bells and whistles ... I treasured it, but when compared to finding my sisters, it was an easy decision to sell the car to pay the investigator."

The Mullings Family 1985

Emily was the first to be found. After being contacted by the private investigator, her adoptive mother called Emily. "Sit down," she said. "I want to tell you something. How would you like to meet your real blood family?" Emily nearly passed out from excitement. "I couldn't take a breath," she remembers. She had always known she was adopted and, growing up the only child in a good family, had wished she had siblings. Now, she did!

Emily's husband, Roger Mullings, was retiring from the Navy that year and they had three sons, ages 16, 13, and 8. Stationed in Chesapeake, Virginia, the Mullings family had contemplated moving to Florida after Roger retired, but

Pensacola had been on their radar, not Ocala. Now, lo and behold, they had family in Ocala!

On the same day she found out about her brothers and sisters, Emily made a three-way long-distance call to Ben and Jean that lasted an hour, and on Valentine's Day, February 14, 1985, she stepped off the plane in the Orlando Airport and into the arms of her long-lost family. "Harry, Ben, Stacy and I were there waiting," recalls Jean. "That's when you could be right there when they got off the plane. We just surrounded her. It was a group hug for sure. She didn't know what to think!"

Jean, Emily and Ben
Reuniting at Orlando Airport

One memorable moment among many in that emotion-filled reunion with their baby sister, Clyde Dean (Emily), was slated to become a family joke. That was the moment when Stacy's then-husband, Jon, upon meeting Emily for the first time, said, "Oh, you must be the one they sent out for bread and moved while you were gone ..." he said, grinning. Everyone in the family laughed, including Emily, who was soon to be known for her sense of humor. In fact, playing it up to the hilt, the family later presented Emily with a pin made especially for her ... with a slice of bread pictured on it!

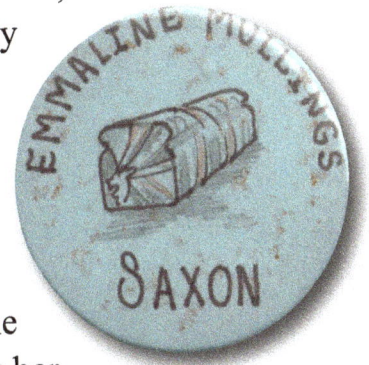

On a pretty spring day in March of 1985, Paula Woodall Manning was working outside in her yard in Tallassee, Alabama when her husband came out and told her there was someone from some adoption agency on the phone and they said her biological family was looking for her. They wanted her permission to give the family her phone number and address. Yes! Her answer was instant, even though her husband and her adoptive mother were both suspicious of this possible intrusion into her life by "strangers" she'd never even met. "I had always known I was adopted and my adoptive mother was real protective," says Paula. "She couldn't have children and I think they were in their fifth year of trying to adopt a child and had just about given up hope when they found me, so I was always told I was 'special' and 'chosen.' They didn't want me to think of anyone as my parents except them." Paula had definitely been treasured, but never encouraged to look into the origin of her birth. Her adopted father, who had spoiled her and given her everything she wanted, was gone now and Paula's husband and adoptive mother were worried. They were in agreement that this "family reunion thing" was not good. Nevertheless, two days later when her husband answered the phone and told her resentfully that there was a man asking for her, Paula was thrilled to the bone to hear that man say, "This is Ben Saxon, your brother."

Paula couldn't wait to meet her family. "I packed my duds and left the next day!" She piled her two young daughters, Petrina and Pollyanna, in the car with her and headed for Ocala - an eight hour drive from Tallassee. On that first trip, she met only Ben and Jean, as Emmett couldn't afford to come down and Emily was still in Virginia with her family. "I stayed three days with Ben and the reason I didn't stay longer was that my adopted mother had really convinced my husband that this was a bad thing; that I didn't know these people. He demanded I come home. He was very jealous and controlling. We had only been married for about ten weeks, so I went back home. My sister Emily called me and we talked back and forth from March through July when we all finally met in Ocala. She had changed her name from Clyde Dean to Emmaline and she was four years older than me, but we had been adopted at about the same time. We found out we had a lot in common. We even look alike!"

The two "found" sisters talked at length about their adoption stories and their earliest memories. "I don't know whether I remember it or dreamed it or just heard the story so many times that I can see it in my mind, but when my adoptive parents got the call that they had a child for them, the agency people brought me out into the room and advised them to spend some time with me and see if they wanted me," says Paula. "They pointed out that I had a crooked nose (a deviated septum), but my parents told them, 'We don't care about her nose. We want her.' I can still see myself in that room."

Paula's adoptive parents are now deceased, but she remembers them fondly, even her adoptive mother, who "wore the pants in the family" and was the one who disciplined her. "My Dad was extremely loving and spoiled me," she says. "I was my Dad's little sweetie. I remember how he would tell me a joke or a story and we'd both be laughing so loud that my Mom would come into the room wondering what in the world was going on. Both of my parents worked very hard to make sure that I always had everything I needed or wanted even if they had to sell a few cows to do it. They surprised me with a new car (a Chevy Nova) for my 16th birthday!" The one thing her parents couldn't get for Paula was the truth about her birth family - that was something that was not discussed in the Woodall household. Paula was their special, chosen daughter and that was that.

In the meantime, back in Ocala, Christine Saxon Sloan had often talked about her missing daughters, wishing that there was some way they could be reunited with her other three children.

"Mother really wanted us to find Clyde Dean and the other baby," recalls Jean. "I did everything I could to help Ben find them because it was important to me, too. I talked to Emmett nearly every day on the phone and was always close to Ben. Harry knew how much we wanted to find them and he helped every way he could, too. "

In July of 1985, the Saxons were reunited at last. The reunion was a joyful one, with all five siblings talking and laughing at once, and a true feeling of accomplishment for Jean, Ben and Emmett. Many photographs were taken of the five siblings, who each bore an unmistakable resemblance to the other four, and a feature article appeared in the Ocala Star Newspaper about the triumphant conclusion to a decades-long search.

Ocala Star Banner – Wednesday, August 14, 1985

PEOPLE

Reunited at last are, from left, Paula Manning, Emmaline Mullings, Ben Saxon, Emmett Saxon, Jr., and Jeannette Acree.

By Becky Watson
Assistant Lifestyles Editor

In the last of the 1940's, a man named Emmett Saxon Sr. left his wife, Christine, and their children – the youngest a baby in arms – looking for a better job.

For Ben Saxon, Emmaline Mullings, Emmett Saxon Jr., Jeannette Acree and Paula Manning, that episode was to change their lives forever.

"Our mother, Christine, was uneducated and didn't have the skills to get a really good job," said Ben. "She depended on her parents and family to help raise her children while she worked."

The three oldest children, Jeannette, Ben and Emmett, kept in touch. Ben was three when he was placed in the Mercy Home in Birmingham, Alabama. Emmett was six. They stayed at the home until they were placed in a foster home

when they were 12 and 14, respectively. Jeannette was in another foster home for a while.

After the years in foster homes, Ben went on to earn a college degree and became more interested in finding his two sisters.

"I really started looking when I was 14 years old," Saxon said, but the letters he wrote to everyone were either unanswered, or the people were unable to help him.

He never lost the desire to find his family, even while raising his own family. He kept thinking about the two lost sisters, talking about them to Jeannette, who also lives in Ocala, and writing Emmett who still lives in Mississippi.

"We would take trips to Alabama, North Carolina, Georgia, all over the place, trying to find information about the two," said Ben. The Mercy Home had no records of the children. He even went to Winter Haven where all of them but Paula were born, but found nothing.

After reading of other area families who had found each other through the help of a private investigator, Ben decided to see if a private investigator could help locate the two women. Emmaline was located in Virginia and Paula in Alabama.

On January 12, Emmaline's adopted mother called and said, "Your brother is trying to locate you." She didn't know she had a brother. Emmaline made arrangements to fly down and visit with Ben and Jeannette.

"We were retiring from the Navy after 21 years so I couldn't get down sooner. Ben's finding me changed my life," said Emmaline. She and husband, Roger, had planned to live in Pensacola after retirement but decided to come to Ocala. "I was going to start looking for the family after we retired, but they found me," she said.

Soon after finding Emmaline, Paula was contacted. "She's our half sister but we wanted to find her as badly as Emmaline," said Ben. "Emmaline had been given some information about Paula by the adoption agency, and at least knew her name. Paula now lives in Tallassee, Alabama with her family. She was not aware of others at all.

They got in touch with Paula on March 13, and she was in Ocala the very next day. She was very excited about finding she had brothers and sisters. In a letter she wrote to Ben she revealed that she could feel the bond between the five siblings. She said it was as though she had always known in her heart there was someone else.

During a weekend in July all of the brothers and sisters and most of their 14 children finally got together at Ben Saxon's home for a giant family reunion.

"There's a few of the kids that couldn't make it," said Emmett, "but there will be other times when we can all get together."

One thing they're grateful for is they are all still young, and have a long time to share their lives together. Ranging in age from mid 3's to mid 40's, it has taken 30 years to find everyone, but it was well worth the wait.

They found that several times they had been very close to one another, but never knew it. Emmett has driven his truck right by Emmaline's home, and Emmaline has taken vacations with her family in Florida and has stayed in Ocala never knowing Ben and Jeannette were in the same city.

They also found that they have many things in common, among them a fondness for lemon pie.

"One thing I wish is that our mother could have lived to see all of us together again," said Ben. "She died in 1980. She was always telling me she wanted to get all the children together again, but didn't know how. She wanted me to try and do that."

They would all like to see the laws changed to allow adopted children to learn more about their natural parents. It would be nice for records to be opened after the person turns 18, they say. Now they just want to get to know each other and relish the newly found sense of family.

Helen, Loressa and Emmett

And get to know each other they did. Harry and Jean and their children, Bruce, Sissy (Dianna) and Stacy, did all they could to make their newly found sisters (aunts) feel welcomed into the family. Emmett, his wife, Helen, and their daughter, Loressa Jeannette, came to Ocala that July and stayed with Harry and Jean for several days, celebrating this huge milestone in their lives. Ben, his wife, Kathy, and their children, Robert and Meredith, hosted the majority of the family gatherings that July, and provided sleeping accommodations for both Emily and Paula, as well as their families. Emily, Roger and their boys, Glenn, Michael and Scott, had such a good feeling about Ocala and their ready-made family there that they decided to retire in that Florida town rather than in Pensacola. Paula, her new husband, Larry Manning, and her daughters, Petrina and Pollyanna, visited for a short time before returning to Tallassee, Alabama. Paula's sons, Rex and Dennis, didn't make it to the family reunion because they were with their father at the time, but Paula knew her life was changed for the better, and when she returned from that first reunion, she wrote a letter to Ben from her heart. The letter, dated 3-21-85, reads

Dear Ben,

I am still so excited about having brothers and sisters. I think of my new found family constantly. There is a bond between us that I feel has been in my heart for as long as I can remember.

Well, I cried most of the way home. I couldn't stand leaving you. But I think you could figure that out for yourself. I was really torn between a new kind of love for my husband and the need and love for my family that I just knew had to be out there somewhere. I was really overwhelmed by it all. Things here are just fine now. Larry and I have talked and talk and talk – so have Mama and I. I feel a lot of good has come out of the talks. They are both right by my side.

Larry had bought me a beautiful large house plant basket that I had been wanting, to welcome me home. He's really a very special kind of guy and once you meet him I think you will agree.

The trip home was really uneventful – the girls slept, I drove and dozed, but made it just fine with your prayers I know. I could feel your presence at my side all the way. I got in at about 3 a.m. our time.

Larry called Jerry Milner Tuesday from work and made an appointment for Wed. I didn't even know he was going to do it but he knew how important it was to me. He said he just wanted to make me happy, but didn't want to find out things that might hurt me. Well this is how the meeting went.

I met Jerry and he was who I thought he was (the guy from Tallahassee) Larry had also gone to high school with him. He recognized Larry. I was not allowed to see the folder (my folder). He told me that mother had married a Saxon in 1940 – had four children. During this time they had lived in both Alabama and Florida – especially the last few years of their marriage. Then he deserted her and the children. She was then living in Alabama with our Grandfather at the time. The four of ya'll were taken away from her. She tried very hard to get ya'll back. In 1951 she became pregnant with me – she had remarried. So Jerry says that she said, but he does not believe this to be true. Her story was that she had remarried but had become pregnant by someone else. She said this husband had also left her – and to the best of Jerry's knowledge of what mother said she only lived with the man about five months. At this time, she was living back and forth from Florida and Alabama. She told Pensions & Security that my father's last name (Green) knew nothing of her pregnancy – that he was a heavy drinker – 5'8" tall, medium build, dark wavy hair, gray eyes and dark skin. He was married to someone else at the time and had two daughters. He could have been from Alabama, Florida or anywhere else for that matter. Jerry Milner is very convinced that this story is not true. He said people in this situation rarely tell the truth. He feels as you do that with my name being Saxon on my birth certificate that there's a great possibility that I am a Saxon, that with the chance of him coming to see mother frequently over the years is very possible, and that mother is the only one who knows. So I guess we are back where we started. Larry feels that since mother had my name Baby Saxon and her name Christine Fleming Saxon as mother that I am a Saxon, but who knows. All I know is that I love all of you very much, and that's all that really matters to me.

I got a letter from Emmaline. It was great to hear from my sister. She sent a few snapshots of her and the kids.

I hope to see all of you soon. Larry and I are trying to plan something soon. His next days off are at Easter which is a bad weekend for a trip for all of us. I will probably have talked to you before you received this letter.

Tell everybody hi! Pollyanna is writing to Robert and Meredith soon.
I love you,
Your sister Paula

as follows:

Just as with all families, some siblings are closer than others and, because Emmett and Paula were in neighboring states, they visited one another a few times, while the three who remained in Ocala stayed in more constant contact.

"The main thing is that we know each other now," says Jean. "It was a relief after all those years of searching. Even to this day, living in the same town, Emily and I rarely visit, but I know if I need her or Paula, they'll help me in a heartbeat. That's what family does."

Emma Kent Fleming (Christine's Mother)
Little boy up front wearing glasses is Uncle Hoyt.

Family Album

(l-r) Jetta Carlos, Clyde Dean Norwood, Grandmother Julia Hudspeth Saxon, Curtis Eli Saxon, and Ben Saxon (age 21)

Uncle Johnny and Pop

Christine's Sister Betty

Drawn by Emmaline Emily Clyde Dean Saxon

The SAXON name is mine by birth
A gift from God to be
Handed down from heaven above
And from my father to me

More honorable men there could never be
Valor, perseverance and generosity
Sturdy as an oak with fortitude
A love of God and country, too

Guardians of all sacred things
And pride of family too
Health, happiness and prosperity
Our forebearers lives show through

Now my child this name is yours
Keep it near your heart
Remember the pride that you feel inside
And never let it depart

Emily's poem

Saxon Siblings

Jean,
Ben
& Emily

Jean and Ben's Stein

Jean, Ben & Paula

The Glamour Sisters
Emily & Jean

Three Sisters Reunited
Paula, Jean & Emily

Jean Saxon Acree

Harry and Jean Acree

Bruce, Jean and
Dianna (Sissy)

90

Harry and Jean,
25th Wedding
Anniversary

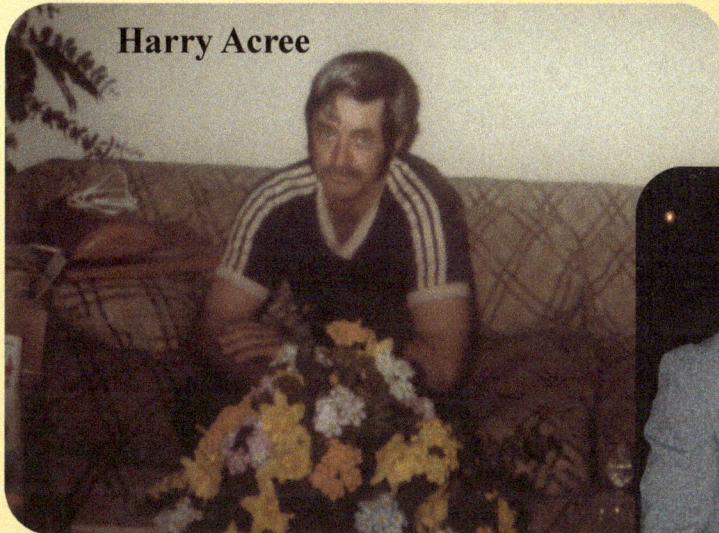

Harry Acree

Harry and
his mother Juanita

Harry's sister Diane,
Juanita & Jean

Jean's Employee of the Year Award, 2002-2003

Harry Acree

Stacy and Bruce

Sissy and Bruce

Sissy, Bruce & Stacy

Bruce Wayne Acree

Bruce, wearing Uncle Ben's Cap and Gown May 1969

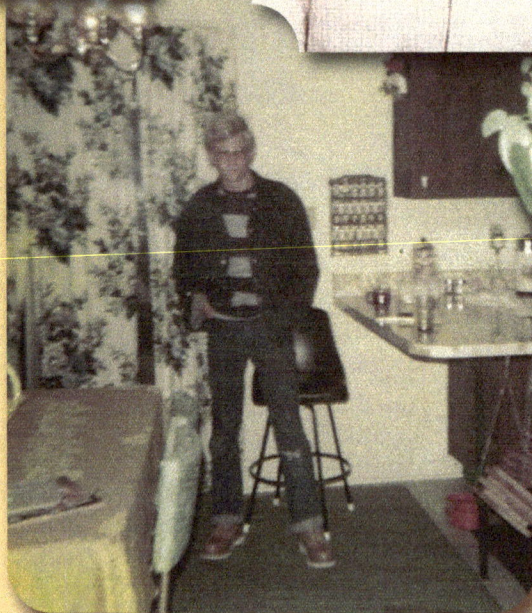

Dianna Lynn Acree Steppen
"Sissy"

Sissy's husband
Thomas Peter Steppen,
business owner and contractor

Thomas &
Sissy's
daughter
Katie Jean
Steppen

Sissy and wedding party

Stacy Lee
Acree Vining

Stacy & Jean

Jon and Stacy,
Wedding Day

97

Joshua Randal Vining,
son of Stacy Lee Acree
& Jon Randal Vining

Handmade
by God

Florida Hospital Waterman

JOSHUA RANDAL VINING
December 4 2004
6 LBS   1 OZ

Class of 2010

Emmett Richmond Saxon, Jr.

Emmett at his church -
a good man with a generous heart

Helen, Loressa & Emmett

Emmett –
always loved,
never forgotten.

In Loving Memory Of

Emmett Richmond Saxon, Jr.
1943 - 2010

A Child of God
and His Faithful Servant

*For God so loved the world, that
he gave his only begotten Son, that whosoever
believeth in him should not perish,
but have everlasting life.*
JOHN 3:16

CrossPointe Fellowship

Ben Lee Saxon

**Ben & Tippie
Ocala, Nov. 1959**

Page in Washington D.C., 1961

**Ben & His Rabbits
at Rodeheaver Boys Ranch, 1962**

**Graduate, Seabreeze High
School, Daytona Beach**

Meredith sees Robert for the first time

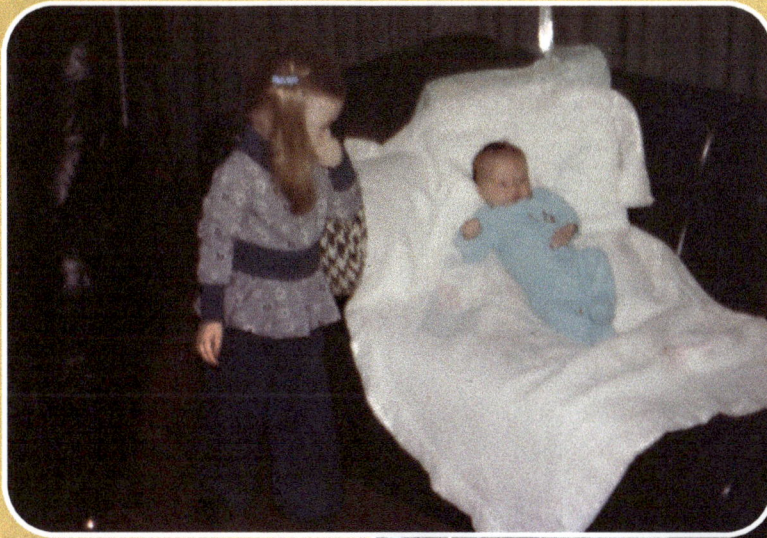

**Meredith holds her
baby brother Robert**

Ben, Robert and puppy

**Graduation Day
Master Degree with Honors, 1980
with Meredith and Robert**

Robert, Ben
& Meredith
in Ben's Classroom

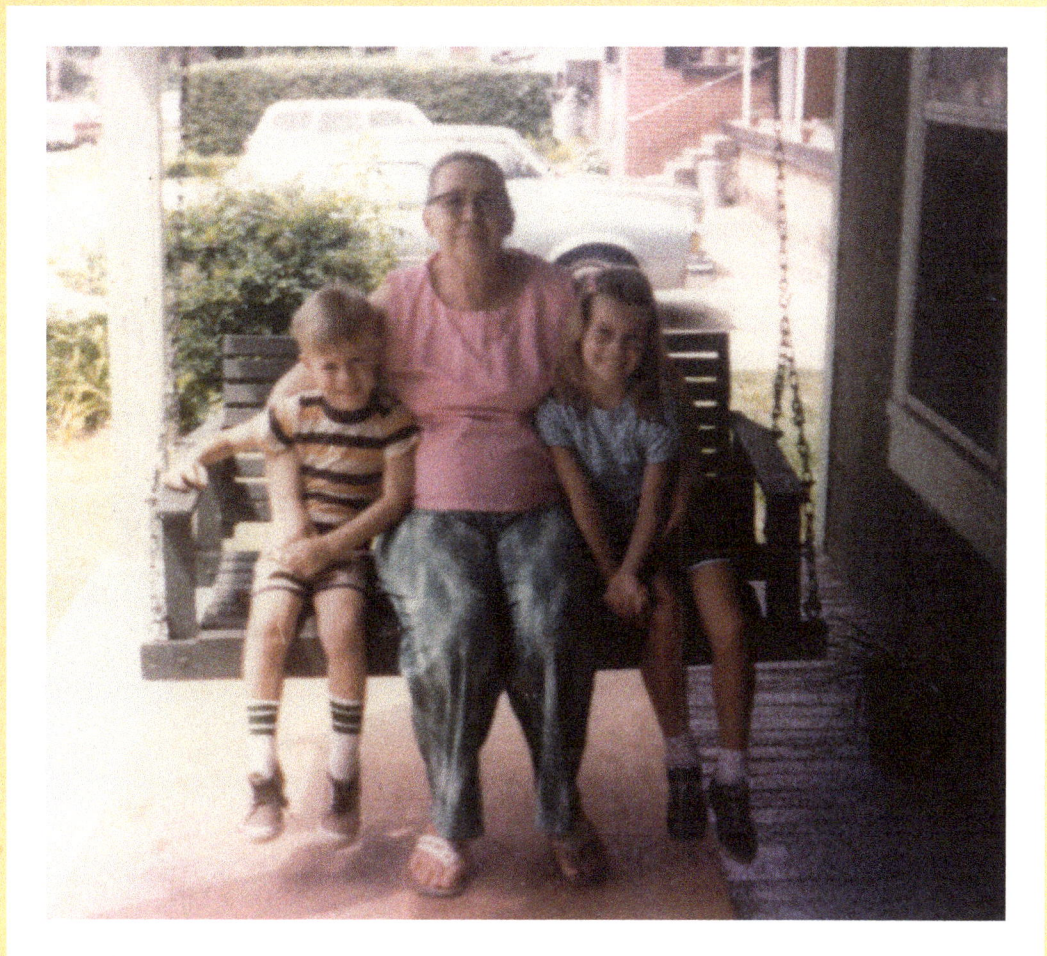

Robert, Christine and Meredith
1980, Warrior, Alabama

**Ben, Emily &
Aunt Jetta Carlos
(father's sister)**

**Robert and
Meredith**

**Robert's High School
Graduation
Ben, Robert, Kathy,
Meredith**

**Ben,
Meredith
and Robert
on Meredith's
Wedding Day**

**Ben
with grandchildren
Michael, Ava
& Isabelle**

Robert Tremaine Saxon

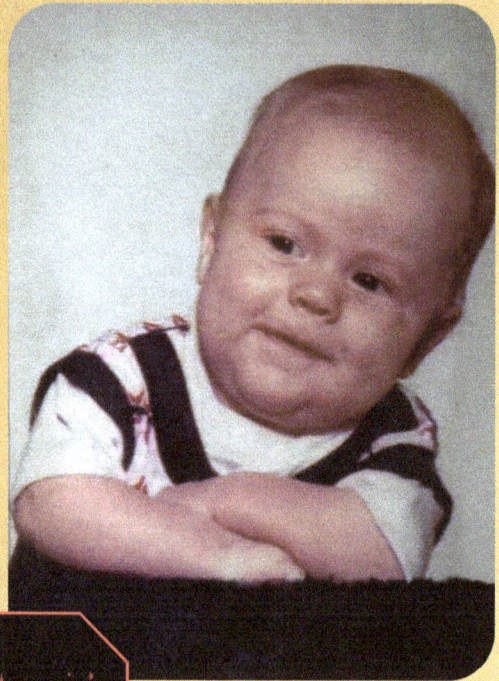

Altar Boy at Grace Episcopal School

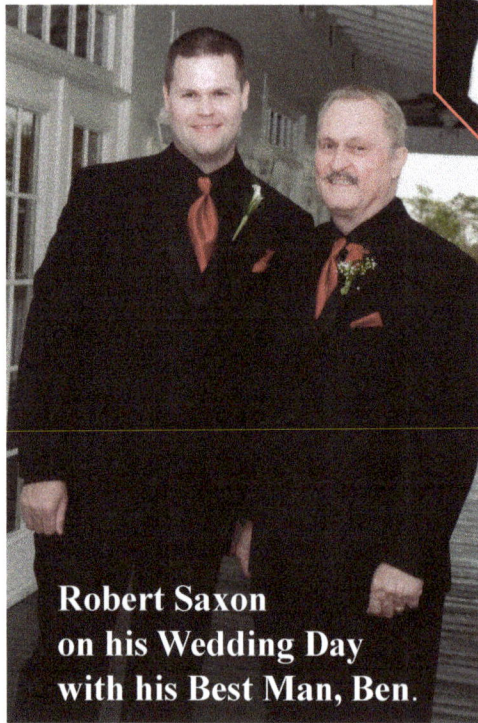

Robert Saxon
on his Wedding Day
with his Best Man, Ben.

Michelle B. Saxon

**Harry, Robert and Jean
Robert's Wedding Day**

**Ben, son Robert
and grandson Mason Lee**

**Mason Lee and
Lauren Grace**

Robert's Family

Meredith Jeannette Saxon

Meredith's 13th Birthday

**Meredith and
Michael Ritacco
Wedding Day**

**Meredith graduates with
master's degree in
speech pathology from
Nova Southern University**

Isabelle and Ava,
Cheerleaders

Isabelle, Michael
and Ava Ritacco

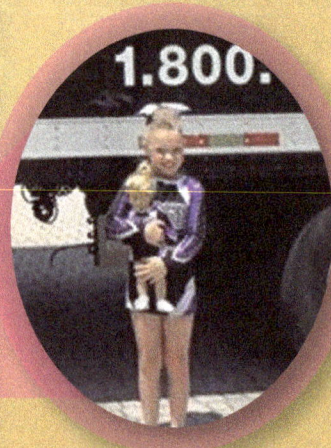

NATIONAL CHEERLEADERS ASSOCIATION

THE WORK IS WORTH IT.®

nca.varsity.com   1.800. NCA.2WIN

1.800.

Isabelle Ritacco

Michael Jr.

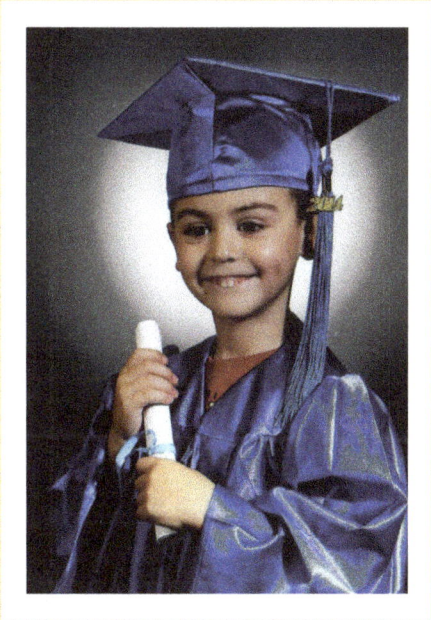

Ava, Meredith,
Michael Jr.
and Isabelle

Photo Collage of Ben's Grandchildren

PRESENTATION

This traditional buckskin warshirt is made in the classic Lakota (Sioux) style by a member of the Standing Rock Sioux Tribe from South Dakota. It was presented to Dave WhiteWolf Trezak on Memorial Day 2003 at the Veterans Powwow at Pulaski, TN for exceptional support and honoring of our nations veterans.

Presentation was made by Earl Yona Taylor. Full Blood Eastern Band Cherokee Commander All Nations Warrior Society Cherokee, NC.

It is being presented By Mr. Trezak to Ben Saxon for the benefit of his family and the youth he teaches in hopes that he will instill in the young people a deeper understanding of the Native Culture in American History. Also to enlighten their minds of the sacrifices of veterans for their personal freedoms Native and Non Native alike.

Dave WhiteWolf Trezak OMAA-10000815933

Dave Whitewolf Trezak was a student of Ben Saxon in Middle School in Ocala, Florida. His respect for his teacher is reflected in this gift.

**Teaching Coach
"History Alive"
San Francisco,
California
2002**

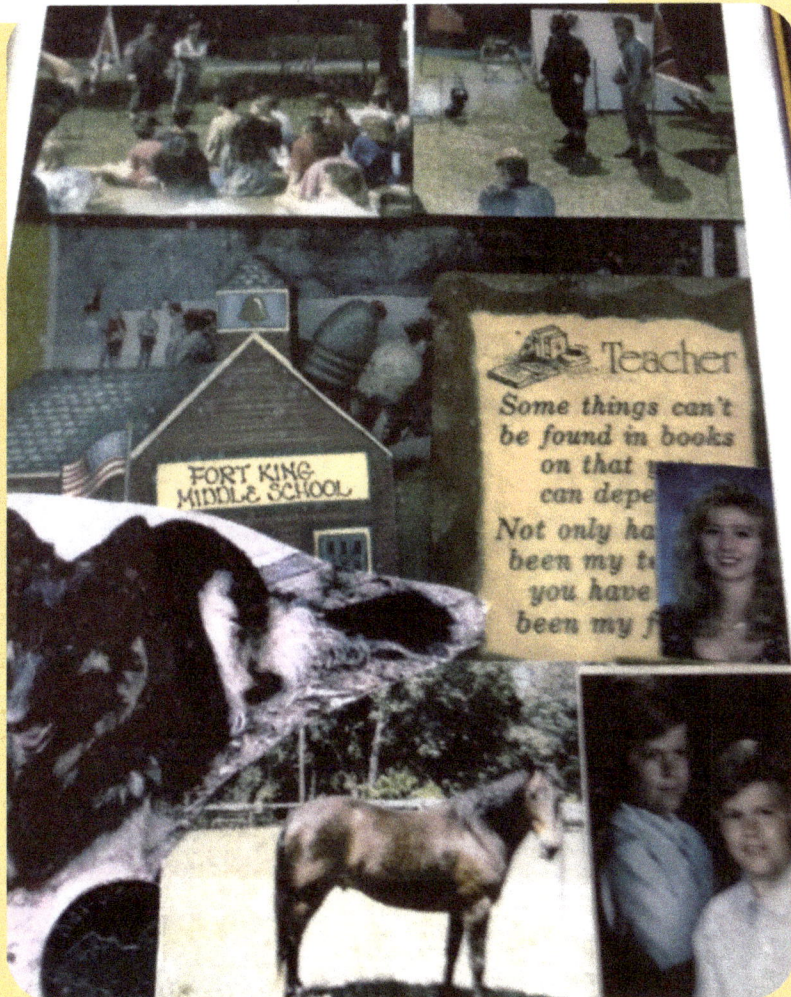

Christonya Brown • Shannon Royster • Mary Ann Ellis • Stephanie Alfeldt • Lynn Casey • Chad Fleig • Victoria Giersbacher • Randi Gibson • Kathleen Alberts • Nancy Cope

Danny Greene • Barbara Denver • Anne Honeycut • Debbie Glawe • Jamie Straib • Jessica Sutton • Jane Palmer • Kathleen Gilbert • Lessie Freeman • Alison Kaminsky

Marcia Trainer • Lori Morgan • Karen McPherson • Michelle Sontag • Ben Saxon • LeAnn Lawler • Cherie Schafer • Mary Van Buren • Rick Corwin • Linda Song

Roxane Edgerina • Barbara Weaver • Joe Ramirez • Jean Krotky • Heather Cox • Mike Mulkey • Gloria Tibbetts • Amy Major • Betsy Gonzales • Caren Burroughs

Josie Rivera • Ra Eckman • Jay Nieto • Jackie Kuffle • Nancy Witt • Dan Perugini

COACHES CAMP
Stanford University, California • 2002

Ben's Collage of Memories

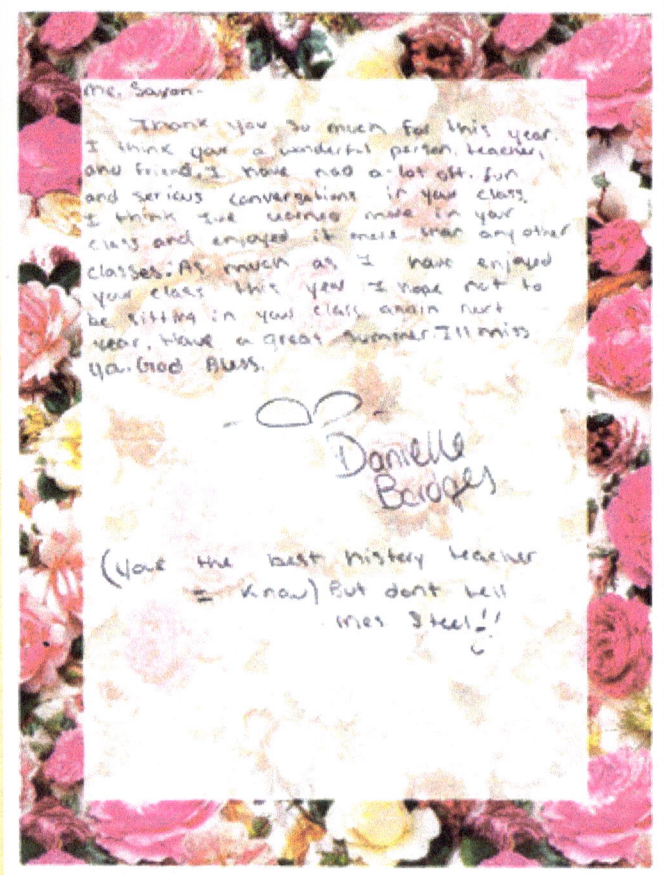

Mr. Saxon-

  Thank you so much for this year.
I think your a wonderful person, teacher,
and friend. I have had a-lot of fun
and serious conversations in your class.
I think I've learned more in your
class and enjoyed it more than any other
classes. As much as I have as I have enjoyed
your class this year I hope not to
be sitting in your class next
year. Have a great summer. I'll miss
you. God Bless.

Danielle
Borgas

(Your the best history teacher
I know) But don't tell
Mrs. Steele!!

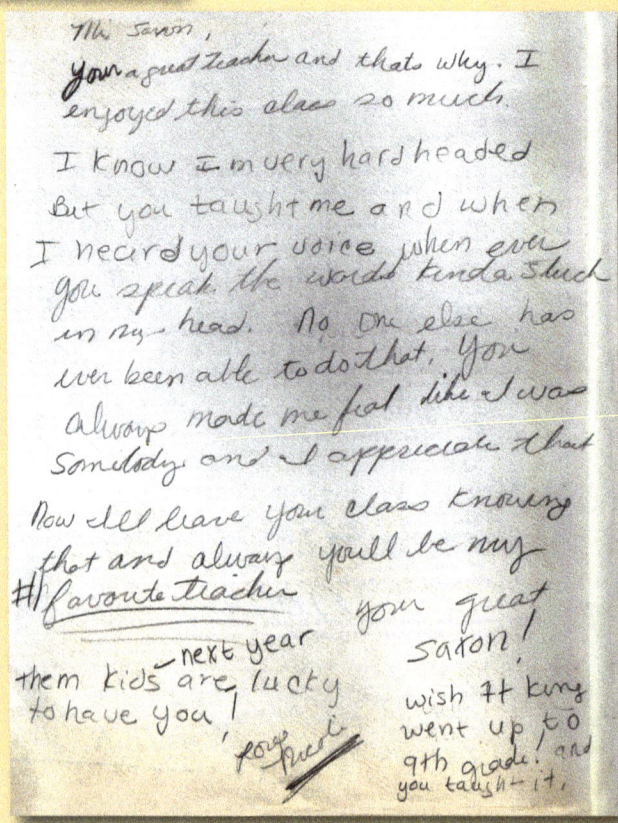

Mr. Saxon,
Your a great teacher and that's why I
enjoyed this class so much.
I know I am very hard headed
but you taught me and when
I heard your voice when ever
you speak the words kinda stuck
in my head. No one else has
ever been able to do that. You
always made me feel like I was
Somebody and I appreciate that.
Now I'll leave your class knowing
that and always you'll be my
#1 favorite teacher.

your great
Saxon!

them kids next year are lucky
to have you!

Love
Nicole

wish Ft. King
went up to
9th grade! And
you taught it.

116

Ocala Chapter Of DAR Announces

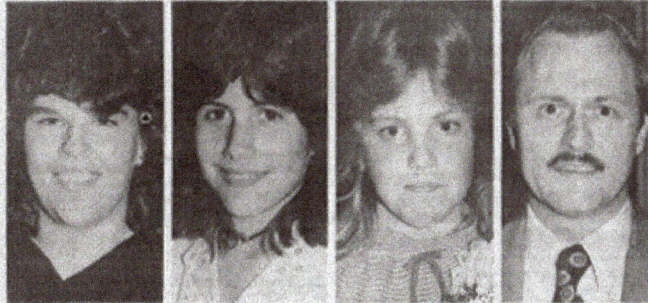

Lori Furrow   Paige Cannon   Dee Richardson   Ben L. Saxon

American History Essay Winners

By MARY ANN MURDOCH
Staff Writer

The local chapter of the Daughters of the American Revolution gathered recently to honor the young winners of its annual American History Essay Contest. And it seemed an appropriate time, since Mayor Wayne Rubinas has declared that February be recognized as American History Month.

More than 50 men and women attended the luncheon meeting and enjoyed the presentation of the winners, and the reading of the essays out loud by the authors.

There were 69 entries this year — 37 at the fifth grade level; 12 at the sixth grade level; and 20 at the eighth grade level.

All middle school students were eligible to enter, and they had two topics to choose from: "American Handicrafts 200 Years Ago," or "A Peacemaker In The Treaty Of Paris."

The first place winner in the fifth grade category was Dee Richardson, a student at Oakcrest Middle School. She wrote about Benjamin Franklin, who was integrally involved in the Treaty of Paris — a document signed in 1783 which ended the Revolutionary War.

Paige Cannon, a sixth grader at Fort King Middle School, won first place in her grade category with an essay on "The Importance Of The Blacksmith During The Revolutionary War."

And finally, Lori Furrow, a student at Lake Weir Middle School, was the first place winner in the eighth grade category. She, too, wrote about Benjamin Franklin, and his important role in the initiation of the Treaty of Paris.

All three winners, after reading their essays, received certificates of appreciation, signed by local DAR chapter regent Dorothy Clark. They also received medals, and a gift from the DAR.

All essay contestants received certificates of appreciation, and were encouraged to enter the contest again next year.

In addition to the student awards, the DAR presented Ben L. Saxon an award for "Outstanding American History Teacher." Ben, an Ocala resident, has been a teacher at Fort King Middle School since 1969.

He has been one of the judges of the DAR essays for several years, and encourages his students to take part in the contest each year.

This year's contest begins in September, and students have until the middle of December to complete their essays, and enter them in the contest. They are judged locally, and then those chosen to compete are judged on the state level. Exact deadlines for this year's contest have not been established, but information can be obtained from the DAR, and from schools.

Recognition for a job well done.

117

Saxon Warriors

As an American history teacher, Ben values the contribution and sacrifice that soldiers and their families have made. The Saxon family has bravely served in many battles. This and the next two pages are dedicated to some of those warriors.

Photo Courtesy of
Roxsanne Wells-Layton, June 2006

Pvt James M. Saxon

Birth: unknown
Death: Dec. 3, 1863

Enlisted as a Private in the 9th Louisiana Infantry, Company D, at the age of 25 years. Wounded on November 7th at Rappahannock Station, VA. Listed as POW on November 7th, 1863 at Rappahannock Station, VA. Died of wounds on December 3, 1863.

James Saxon was wounded and captured at Rappahannock Station, Virginia on November 7, 1863. His leg was amputated. On December 3, 1863 the ligature separated from his femoral artery and he lost so much blood that he died eight hours later. Saxon's case is detailed in the Medical and Surgical History of the Civil War. His headstone incorrectly states he died on December 4 — that was the day he was buried as he died on December 3, 1863.

Although he was in a Louisiana regiment he was from Cuthbert, Randolph County, Georgia. He had ten brothers and sisters.

Burial:
Arlington National Cemetery
Arlington County, Virginia, USA

SAXON, JAMES M
D 9 LA INF
BURIED AT: SECTION CONF SITE 226
ARLINGTON NATIONAL CEMETERY

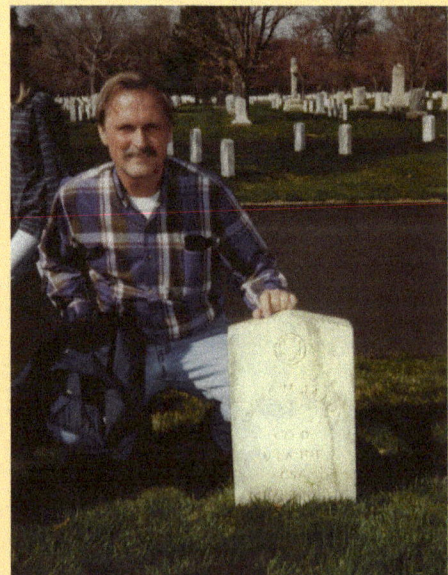

Ben Saxon honors the grave of
Pvt. James M. Saxon on March 26, 1995

LCpl Clyde Edward "Pop Corn" Saxon

Birth:
Sep. 6, 1949
Jenkins County,
Georgia, USA

Death:
Mar. 18, 1969
Quang Nam,
Vietnam*

CLYDE EDWARD SAXON
is honored on Panel 29W, Row 73 of the Vietnam Veterans Memorial.

Wall Name:	CLYDE E SAXON
Date of Birth:	9/6/1949
Date of Casualty:	3/18/1969
Home of Record:	WAYNESBORO
County of Record:	BURKE COUNTY
State:	GA
Branch of Service:	MARINE CORPS
Rank:	LCPL
Panel/Row:	29W, 73
Casualty Province:	QUANG NAM

Clyde was the son of Lewis Saxon of Keysville GA, he enlisted in the US Marine Corps on May 7, 1968 in Waynesboro GA. He arrived in Vietnam on October 24 and was assigned for duty with Company G, 2d Battalion, 7th Marines, 1st MARDIV (Rein) FMF.

While on patrol in the vicinity of Hoi Vuc hamlet north of Hill 35 in Hieu Duc District the Marines received a volley of small arms fire and grenades that wounded two of their comrades. Returning fire, supporting mortar fire was requested as well as a MEDEVAC for the wounded. When the helicopters arrived, two were shot down by the enemy fire as the fire fight continued with the opposing forces. By the time the enemy broke contact and withdrew two Marines had been killed in the action, LCpl Saxon was one of those men, he had died as a result of an enemy gunshot wound.

LCpl Saxon was presented with the Silver Star Medal posthumously "For conspicuous gallantry and intrepidity in action ....on 18 March 1969...."

(Published in THE TRUE CITIZEN, Waynesboro, Georgia, March 26, 1969 – PAGE 2)

L/Cpl. Clyde E. (Popcorn) Saxon, 19, was killed in action in Vietnam March 18. Platoon Radioman in Golf Company, he sustained a gunshot wound to the body.

He enlisted in the Marine Corps in May, 1968, received his basic training at Parris Island, S.C., and left Camp Le Jeune, N.C., Sept. 29. 1968 for duty in Vietnam. Prior to military service he was employed at the Deloach Shopping Center and Samson Manufacturing Compnay.

Survivors include his father and stepmother, Mr. and Mrs. Lewis Saxon, Keysville; his mother, Mrs. Alice McDaniel of Glenville; paternal grandmother Mrs. Idell Lovett Saxon of Waynesboro, maternal grandmother, Mrs. Jack Lowe, Glenville; one sister, Miss Tresa Saxon, Keysville, one brother George E. Saxon, Keysville.

Burial: Millen City Cemetery, Millen, Georgia, USA
- *Plot: Section C, Lot 335*
- *GPS (lat/lon): 32.80534, -81.93093*

Scraping from the Vietnam Veterans Memorial Wall

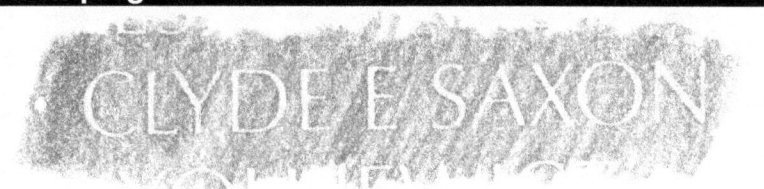

CLYDE E SAXON

PVT. Richmond "Richard" Nally Saxon
Co. E 3rd Georgia Infantry

Birth: Jan. 5, 1817 in Bleckley Co., GA
Death: Dec. 3, 1891 ib Randolph Co., GA

Richmond Nally SAXON was a son of Henry SAXON (1775-1856) and his first wife Judith SMITH (she died ca 1832 in GA, he in 1856 in Leon Co., FL, where he lived with second wife Elizabeth OLIVER).

The gate at the Martin Cemetery only shows that he laid the fence that encloses the graves of his first wife Margaret Jane Martin Saxon, their daughter Nancy J. Saxon and son James M. Saxon. Richmond Nally Saxon was buried next to his second wife. She died a few months before him.

Spouses: First wife: Margaret Jane Martin Saxon (b.1823 - d.1865)
         Second wife: Sophia Jane Bass Saxon (b.1824 - d.1891)
Burial: New Bethel Cemetery Cuthbert
          Randolph County, Georgia

Created by: Brenda A. Darbyshire
Record added: Mar 24, 2010
Find A Grave Memorial# 50170910

NOTE:
37th Regiment Georgia Volunteer Infantry. This regiment was formed by the consolidation of the **3rd Battalion Georgia Volunteer Infantry** and the **17th Battalion Georgia Volunteer Infantry** by S.O. #171, A&IG) (20 July 1863). When the regiment was formed the officers wanted to call it the 1st Georgia Volunteers but Confederate officials in Richmond objected to this request and the designation was changed to the 37th Regiment Georgia Volunteer Infantry. Many of its members were from Murray, Jackson, Franklin, Elbert, and Hall counties. The unit was assigned to General Bate's,

Tyler's, and J.A. Smith's Brigade, Army of Tennessee. It fought with the army from Chickamauga to Atlanta, endured Hood's winter campaign, and was active in North Carolina. The 37th lost fifty percent of the 391 engaged at Chickamauga and in December, 1863, totaled 416 men and 265 arms. Few surrendered on April 26, 1865. The field officers were Colonel A.F. Rudler; Lieutenant Colonel Joseph T. Smith; and Majors Jesse J. Bradford, Meredith Kendrick, and R.E. Wilson.

Margaret Jane Martin Saxon
First Wife of Richmond Nally Saxon

Birth: Jan. 26, 1823 in Shady Dale, Georgia (Jasper County)
Death: Sep. 25, 1865 in Randolph County Georgia

Wife of Richmond Nally Saxon, dtr. of James Martin & Hester Bogan. Many family members in cemetery. (Graves of Margaret, dtr Nancy J and son James M are fenced together - with wrought iron - Bronze gate marker "R.N. Saxon")

Family links:
 Parents:
  James Martin (1788 - 1869)
  Hester Bogan Martin (1789 - 1867)

Spouse:
  Richmond "Richard" Nally Saxon (1817 - 1891)

Children:
  James M Saxon (1839 - 1840)*
  Nancy J Saxon (1844 - 1863)*

Siblings:
  Isaac Martin (1812 - 1888)
  Robert Martin (1814 - 1899)
  Esther Bogan Martin Houston (1819 - 1905)
  Margaret Jane Martin Saxon (1823 - 1865)
  Samuel Crawford Martin (1825 - 1903)
  George Washington Martin (1829 - 1915)**Half-sibling
  James Caswell Martin (1839 - 1918)

Inscription:
        "Dear is the spot where Christians Sleep"
        "In Memory Of - Consort of R N Saxon"
Burial: Martin Family Cemetery
          Randolph County, Georgia

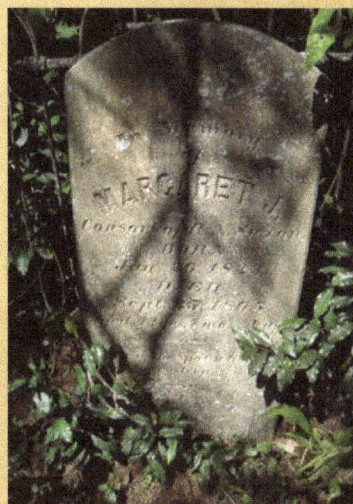

Created by: Gerry Hill
Record added: Nov 19, 2008
Find A Grave Memorial# 31537758

Satana St. Saxon, Ben's first German Shepherd Dog

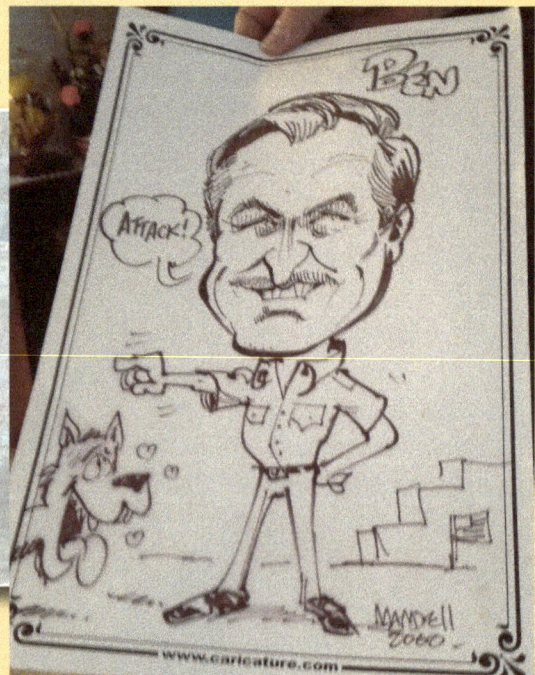

Emily Saxon Scoggins Mullings
(Clyde Dean/Emmaline)

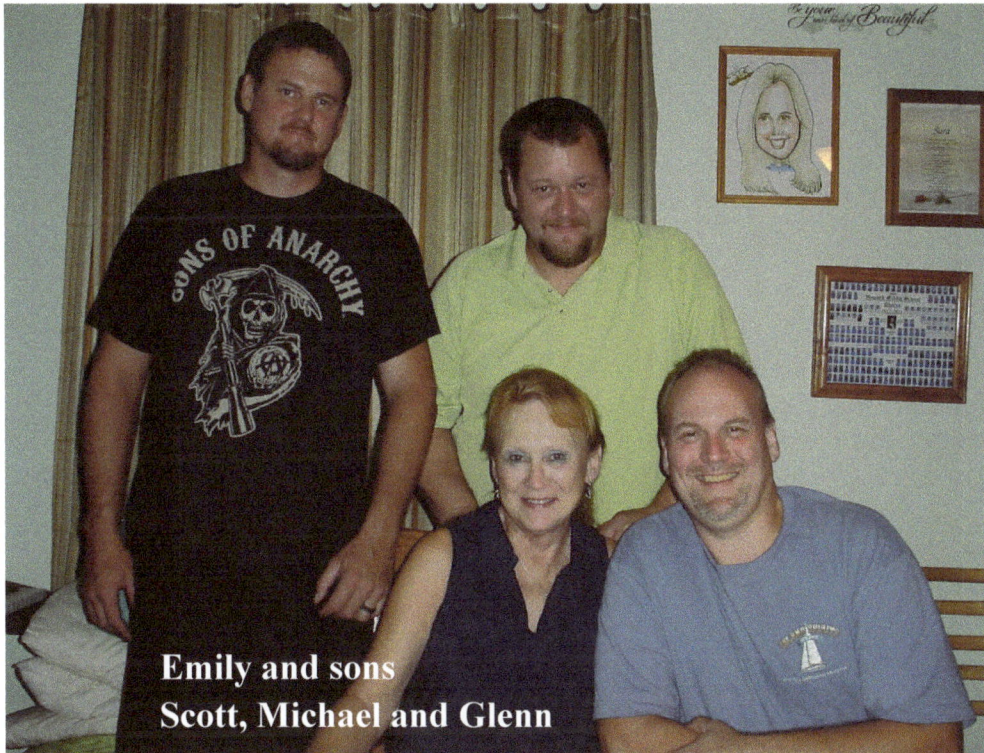

Emily and sons
Scott, Michael and Glenn

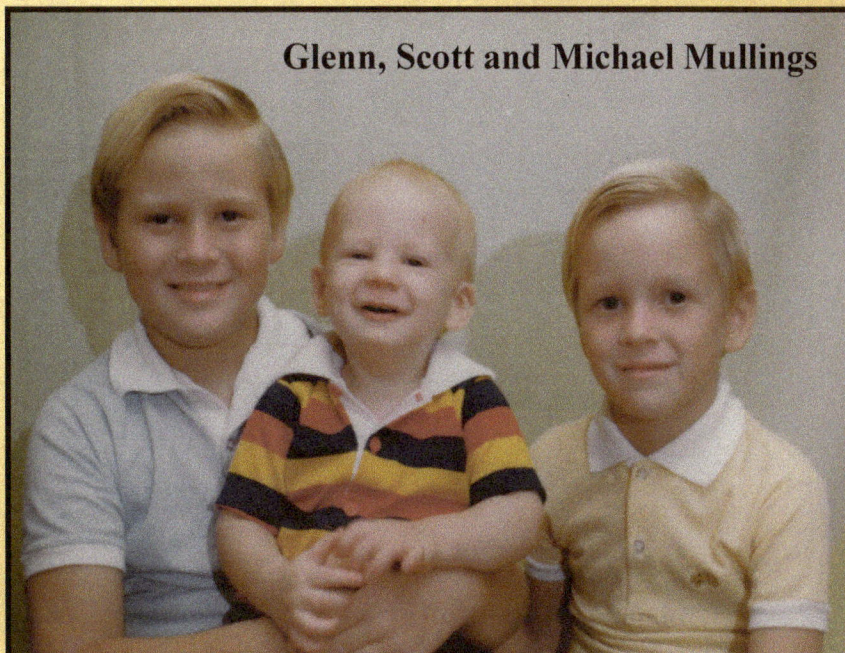

Glenn, Scott and Michael Mullings

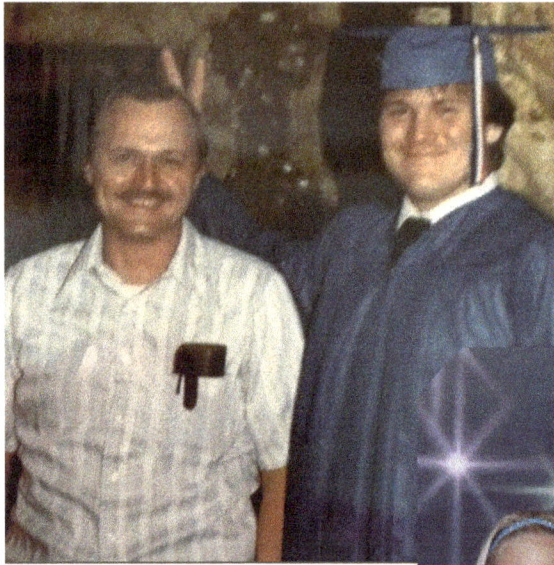

Glenn and his Uncle Ben

Glenn's kids
Brandon Matthew
and Jessica Lee

Glenn, Brandon,
Jessica and Terri

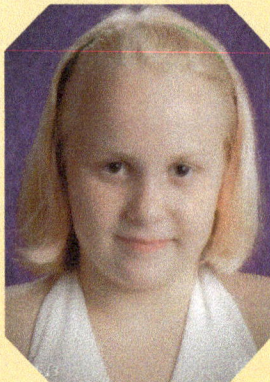

Michael's daughter
Rebecca Madison

Jean, Aunt Joyce
and Emily

Scott's daughter
Sara Elizabeth Mullings

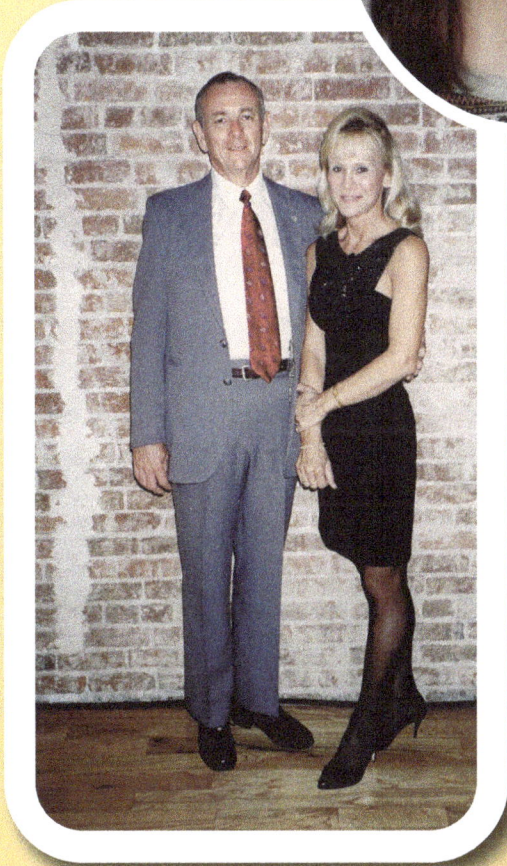

Roger & Emily
20th High School
Reunion

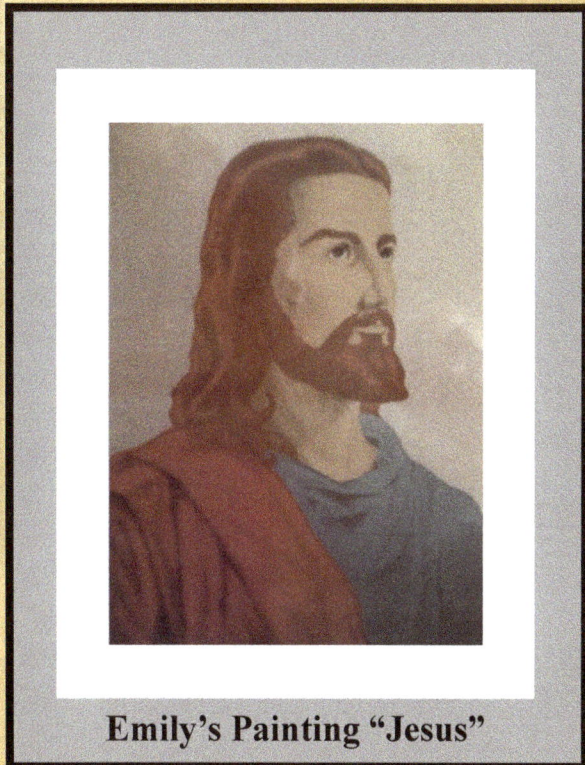

Emily's Painting "Jesus"

Roger, Glenn, Brandon and Edgar Mullings

Four Generations

Juanita, Jessica, Terri & Emily

Paula
Woodall
Manning

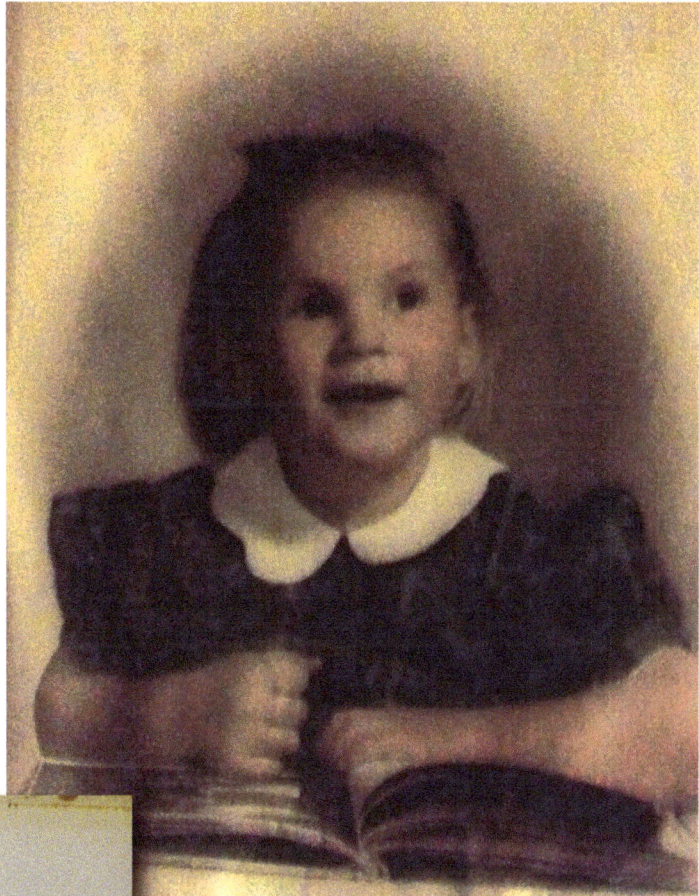

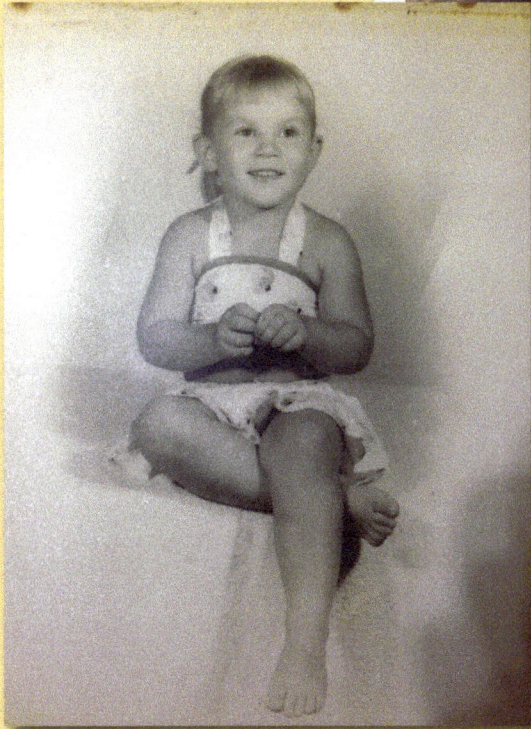

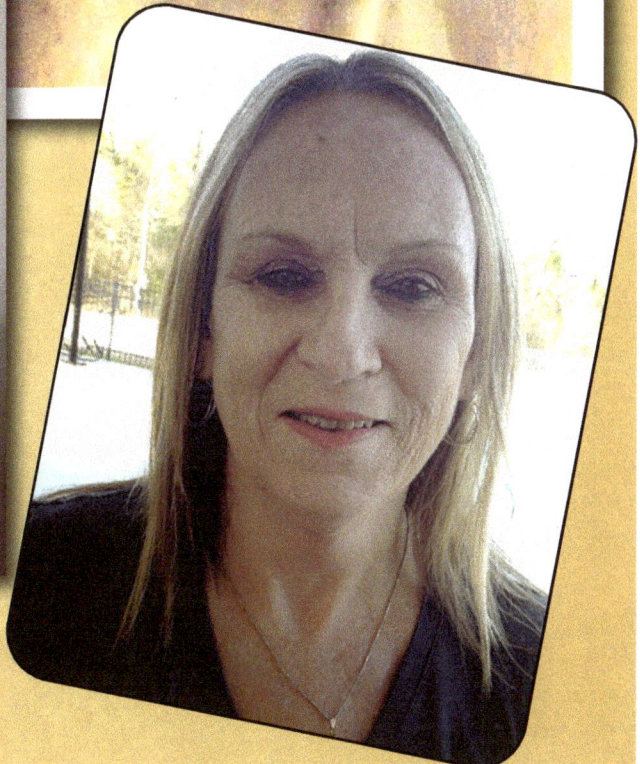

Rex, Dennis, Pollyanna & Petrina

Pollyanna, Petrina, Paula and Emily, 1987

**Alena,
Petrina's daughter**

**Rex's son
Tres Ledbetter**

**Emily Paige,
Dennis' daughter**

**Dennis' son Joshua Paul,
with Ashley and their kids**

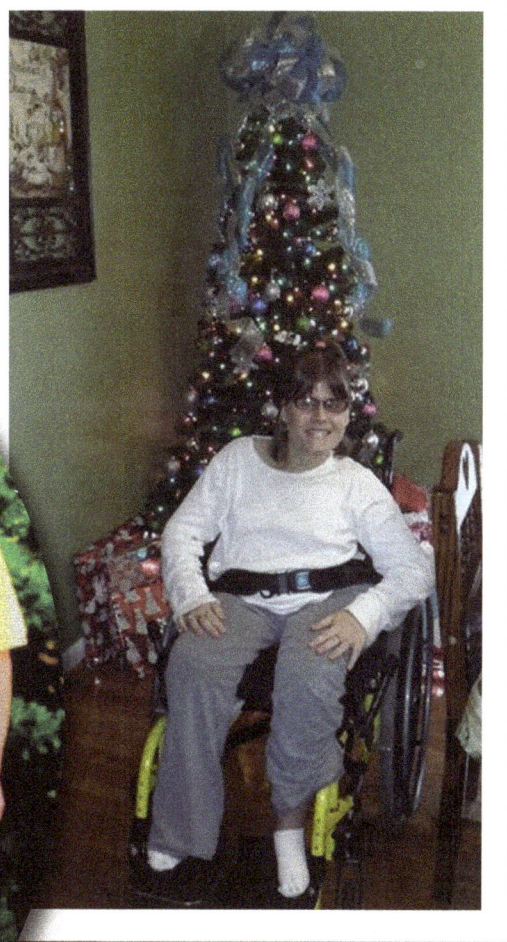

Pollyanna

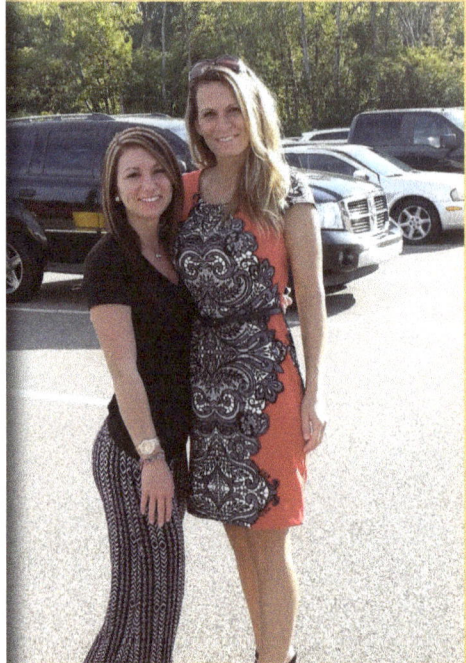

Pollyanna and Alexa at
Koreys Graduation

Petrina

Chris, Payton,
Petrina & Alena

Korey up front with flag,
Graduation Day

Alexa graduates
from dental school

Alexa, Korey, Braden
and John Cade

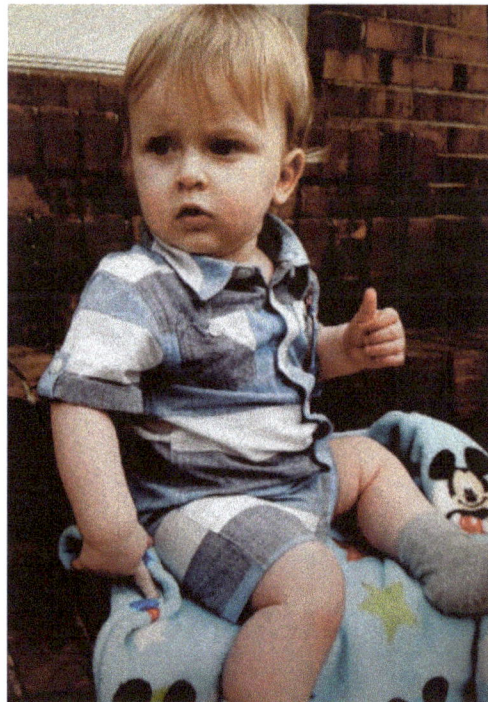

Ayden Spivey, Korey's son

Chapter Eight

Lost No More

After all those years of searching, the Saxon siblings were finally in touch and able to go on living their own lives, knowing in their hearts that their mother's wishes had been fulfilled. In 1985, when they all finally got together, their immediate family numbered 24, with just the five siblings, their spouses, and their children.

Jean and Harry's son, Bruce, was 26, and their daughters, Sissy and Stacy, were ages 23 and 19, respectively. Emmett and Helen's daughters, Loressa and Elizabeth, were ages 16 and 21. Emily and Roger's boys, Glenn, Michael and Scott, were ages 16, 13 and 8. Paula had been married to Larry Manning for just a few months at the time of the reunion. Her four children from her previous marriage, Petrina, Pollyanna, Dennis and RexLedbetter were ages 5, 10, 15 and 16. Ben and Kathy's children, Meredith and Robert, were ages 13 and 11, respectively.

The reunion brought major changes for Emily and Roger and their boys, as they chose to retire in Ocala rather than Pensacola, Florida. For Ben and Jean, Emily's desire to be near her older brother and sister was a wonderful outcome after their years of searching for her. "It would have been great if all five of us could have ended up in the same town," says Jean. "Ben and I really longed for a real family right here with us after all that time of being apart."

While Emmett and Paula both went back to their homes in other states, Emily truly felt like she was home when she was in the loving arms of her siblings. For the first six months, while they secured jobs and found a home to buy in Ocala, Emily, Roger and the boys lived with Ben and his family.

They found they did have much in common, especially a love of animals. The Saxon family of four had one German Shepherd, a medium sized mixed-breed, two cats and a poodle, and the Mullings family of five had a husky and a poodle ... more animals than there were children!

Rachael, Bear, Mandy, Pepi, Nicki

Both Ben and Kathy had busy full-time jobs and the kids were off for the summer break, so Emily became the house mother, temporarily letting the youngsters sleep in until the other adults got up, showered and out the door. "Ben had a bunch of chickens out in a pen in the backyard. I'd go gather eggs before I cooked breakfast for the kids," recalls Emily. "I cooked a lot of goulash and other filling dishes that would stretch for nine people, and the laundry was constant, but when I look back at that time we spent at Ben's house, what stands out is the bonding we did as a family. I wanted to absorb everything I could about my brother and sister, and when Ben and Jean talked about their lives, I'd just try to imagine it. My mouth would just drop open. They were having such a tough time while I was being babied and spoiled. How could that be?"

134

Once in a while, the three siblings would go out with their families to breakfast or lunch at local restaurants and sit reminiscing and enjoying one another's company, "just like a big, happy family," Emily recalls. At home, the five cousins got along well. Emily and Roger were strict but loving, having raised their three boys in the military, and Ben would brook no nonsense either, so it was remarkably peaceful in those extremely close quarters. One of the saving graces that kept the kids occupied that summer was regular attendance at the Boys and Girls Club. "Oh, we had our moments and we bumped into each other once in a while, but all in all, we managed pretty well," laughs Emily.

Laughter, as a matter of fact, was one of the predominant sounds in that house during the time that Emily and Ben combined their families. The antics of the animals provided quite a bit of that hilarity. The two miniature poodles, Peppy and Mandy, got together and produced five tiny multi-colored puppies. Nikki, the Husky, and Rachel, the German Shepherd, spent most of their time competing, each of them vying for dominance. The chickens (Ben's 4-H project for his kids) escaped from the pen one day and, knowing how particular Ben was about his chickens, Emily spent hours rounding them up. When Ben got home and found his little sister out in the yard, exhausted, dirty and sweaty, but triumphant because she'd finally corralled all the chickens, he just burst out laughing. "All you had to do was tell Rachael to round up the chickens and she would have had it done in five minutes," he told her, pointing at his shepherd. "She's a working dog."

Speaking of work, it wasn't long before Roger got on with the custodial department of the Marion County School System, and Emily was left to register the boys for their classes and make sure they had their immunizations and school clothes and everything they needed to start fresh in a new place. This was something she'd done before, as a Navy wife and mother, and it seemed like a typical motherly thing to do until she listened in shock as Ben told her that he had registered himself for school because their mother hadn't cared whether he went or not. Possibly because of the irregularities in his own public school history, and despite the fact that he was a popular middle school teacher in the Marion County School System, Ben chose to put Meredith and Robert in private schools.

Once school started, Emily began looking for a job. By now, Ben, Kathy, Jean and now, Roger, worked for the Marion County School System in one capacity or another, so it seemed logical for Emily to pursue a job there, too. She had attended Southern Business College in Vicksburg, Mississippi after graduation and was an excellent secretary, proficient in shorthand and typing, but when she was offered a job working with children with learning disabilities, she was interested. It turned out to be a wonderfully fulfilling job teaching children to be self-reliant and, hopefully, grow up to get a job to feed their families instead of turning to the government for help. Emily truly enjoyed working with these special-needs children, especially the opportunity to make them feel good about themselves. She had been pampered and made to feel good about herself all through her childhood and she wanted these children to feel the same way. "Every day was a new experience," she says. "For 13 years I worked in a classroom with learning-disabled children – 6th, 7th and 8th graders – and I loved it."

Having been raised in a loving, affectionate home, raising her children in the same sort of home, and then working with children in the school system, Emily had always recognized and valued the power of the human touch. When she got the opportunity to attend the Florida School of Massage in Gainesville and use her strong hands and heart to earn a living, she went for it. "It was Roger's parents who helped fund my massage therapy schooling, which was very expensive, but it was well worth it and I've always been grateful to them for helping me," she says, looking back now at more than 17 years as one of the top massage therapists in Central Florida. Once she became a licensed massage therapist (L.M.T.), Emily partnered with another L.M.T., Julian Alvis Cameron. Together, Emily and Alvis provided the healing touch to many patients over the next 17 years through their practice, Healthwise Therapeutic Massage.

In addition to sharing a profession, Emily and Alvis also shared a passion for country music. Always a poet as well as a musician, Emily combined her writing talent and musical ability to write some country tunes, while Alvis, who had played guitar and sung in a country band in high school, also wrote songs and sang them. The two of them eventually originated their own Kountry Wyse Record Label, LLC, and made some CD's. Over the years, Emily and Alvis were able to attend many country music concerts. The celebrity photos they collected cover the walls of their office vying for wall-space with the many awards and certificates they earned for massage therapy. One of the certificates Emily is proudest of is the one from ARC, commending her massage therapy business for contributing the healing power of massage to developmentally disabled children and adults on a regular basis.

In 1997, Emily's poem, "A Simple Touch" was published in The National Library of Poetry Anthology – *Through the Looking Glass*:

A Simple Touch

It's really very simple this soothing idea of touch
How it can and often does so very, very much

It has such power ... such purpose too
Relaxing, calming, caring and sharing sometimes even revealing
Feelings or thoughts we often keep concealing

Touching gently with hands so firm
Listening quietly for a chance to learn
Tuning in for a glimpse within helping the stressful soul to mend

When muscles relax and nerves unwind
There's a refreshed body – a refreshed mind
A healing energy flows all through
Awakening the senses ... awakening you

So it really is simple this wonderful idea of touch
That it really does so very much
To improve your life ... this "simple touch"

Earning certifications for learning and applying new and innovative massage techniques, and helping promote the benefits of massage therapy, Emily Mullings has made a positive impact in the Ocala community. Unfortunately, in March of 2014, her long-time massage therapy and country music partner, Julian Alvis Cameron, passed away at age 75. Between the death of her business partner, some recent health issues faced by her husband, Roger, and the fact that she and Roger have been responsible for raising their granddaughter, Sara, since she was quite young, Emily has decided to retire in 2015. "When I couldn't be there, Roger was always there for Sara. Now I need to be there for both of them," says Emily.

Jean had started working with the Marion County School System in late 1984 and was already firmly established there when Emily came along. Although all three siblings, Jean, Emily and Ben, served in entirely different capacities within the same school system, there was a common thread woven through the work they did ... compassion. Ben and Jean had grown up without the warmth of love and compassion and now it was part of their daily curriculum. Emily, raised with an abundance of both, emulated her adoptive parents as well as her brother and sister, and passed it on to her students.

When Jean worked with the CTAE (Comprehensive Technical and Adult Education) as a teacher's aide, she set up computers and showed students how to use them, and helped some of them get their high school diplomas. There was a young girl whose work had been rejected by the head teacher and she came to Jean asking if she would take the time to check her papers. When Jean did take the time and worked with the girl, it turned out that she was capable of doing the work after all and had just needed someone to be patient with her. Later, Jean remembers, that same girl came back to proudly show off her wedding ring. "She'd gotten married and she wanted me to know about it because she knew I cared about her," says Jean.

When Jean first began working with school system in 1984, she was teaching disabled adults, helping them do basic skills like making a bed and brushing their teeth, helping them learn to dress properly for an interview, how to inquire about a job, how to fill out a job application, and, basically, how to be a responsible employee. It was a job that required a great deal of patience and repetition, but those were skills Jean had learned early and well. Having repeatedly swept the carpet for Inez back at the Mercy Home as a child, Jean knew about being patient and determined. These were students who were capable of working somewhere, but just needed guidance, and Jean was the one to do it. When they did find employment, Jean would follow up at the job-site to make sure they were there and doing what they needed to be doing. She had the kind of persistence and re-sponsibility that made her a valuable asset to the program. Many of her students were successful in finding permanent employment, and some still come up to her when they see her today to tell her how much they appreciate what she did for them.

Eventually, Jean was asked to teach special needs children through the ARC (Association of Retarded Citizens) Program. "You give them something to do and they're perfectly happy," says Jean, recalling that at first she wasn't sure she had what it took to teach handicapped children, but she discovered the kids liked her and she liked them. They were developmentally disabled or on the lower spectrum of intelligence, mostly, and again, Jean's patience made a big difference. "There was one little black boy named Wilbur who always sat by me at my desk and did his homework," Jean recalls. "We'd talk sometimes and when I asked him what he was having for supper one night, he said, 'Whatever I go home and cook.'" About a year after Wilbur graduated from the program at Vanguard High School, Jean and Harry and Stacy were sitting at an outside table at Sonics in Ocala when a pretty red truck pulled up. "Mom…" said Stacy. Before she could say any more, Wilbur had jumped out of the truck, come up and hugged Jean and gotten back in his truck. He was apparently one of those students who credited her for whatever success he achieved in life – and that included a pretty red truck! There was another young man who was about 6'7" and had a plate in his head from a car accident, but came into the classroom every day and worked as hard as he could to learn whatever he could. "That young man still sends me Mother's Day Cards and Christmas Cards that he does on his computer," says Jean, smiling at the memory of teaching those students in that classroom.

Jean worked for the Marion County Public School District for seventeen years, achieving her goals of security, and also making a positive difference in the lives of countless students. In the 2002-2003 school year, Jean was designated Employee of the Year by the Marion County Public School District. Her glass trophy with her name on it and her picture in the middle of it is gathering dust in the china cabinet, but Jean's memories of those days still sparkle in her eyes when she talks of them.

By the time the siblings found one another in 1985, Ben had been teaching middle school for about 17 years and was a respected member of the Marion County School System as well as the faculty of Fort King Middle School. In 1985, Junior Achievement of America offered to train two Fort King Middle School teachers to work with 8th grade students in the JA Program. The principal chose two 8th grade social studies teachers, Ben Saxon and Eleanor Steele, to train.

The Junior Achievement Program teaches students about goal setting, and how to manage money, including credit cards and interest, how to plan for their careers and in general how to be better prepared for a successful future. Junior Achievement of America brought in leaders from the business community (CPA's, Attorneys, Executives from Lockheed Martin, etc.) to speak with the students, and at the end of the 12-week course, students earned a Junior Achievement Certificate. Ben worked with Junior Achievement for the remainder of his teaching career and won a great deal of recognition from the national organization as a highly successful Junior Achievement teacher and advocate, but that first year, 1985, is one he particularly remembers because it was a year of both achievement and transition for him. The achievement of finally finding his sisters after decades of searching was a gratifying one indeed, and being chosen by his principal to head up a nationally recognized goal-oriented program was another highlight of that year, but 1985 was also a sadly transitional time for Ben and his family because his marriage with Kathy was ending in divorce.

By 1986, Ben had become a single dad with custody of his daughter, Meredith and his son, Robert. Ironically, it was almost as if God had planned that he and Jean would find Emily before Ben's divorce because now he had two sisters living nearby and helping him with his new role as a single dad and, most especially, helping his daughter, Meredith, deal with the changes happening in her life. He not only had two devoted sisters giving him and his kids the love and support they needed to get through this traumatic time, but Jean's husband, Harry, went out of his way to be like the paternal grandfather they had never had. Ben also had the distraction of being the teacher that ran the Junior Achievement Night Company, where students actually learned to create, manufacture and sell items, and the planning for that helped him as well as his students.

Emmett and Paula were supportive, but far away in Mississippi and Alabama, and several times in those early years, Paula remembers that they got together and enjoyed being the brother and sister "on the outside." Emmett, of course, kept in touch with Jean and Harry regularly by phone, and Ben knew that if he needed Emmett's help, all he had to do was call him. They were all now known to one another, thanks to Ben's persistence and his hiring of that private detective, and the fact that they didn't all live in the same town was no barrier to brotherly and sisterly love.

It was during those years after the quest for his sisters ended that Ben embarked on another quest ... this time to discover the Saxon ancestry and verify the bits and pieces of conversation he'd heard all his life about his father, Emmett Richmond Saxon's prominent and important relatives in Tallahassee. The deeper Ben dove into the genealogy of the Saxon family, the more validated he was that he came from people of quality despite the shame and poverty of his childhood. He and Jean and Emmett had always had a defiant sense of self-worth even in the worst of their childhood horrors, and now Ben felt the bold pioneer blood of his paternal ancestors coursing through his body as he researched his heritage. He also knew that his mother had had Indian blood and he could feel that courageous strain stirring in him as well. Gathering proof of ancestry was exciting, and when he had satisfied his academic demand for authenticity, he began sharing what he had discovered with his siblings.

Their father, Emmett Richmond Saxon of Tallahassee, Florida, was a descendant of Samuel Saxon, one of three brothers who came to Virginia from Hampshire, England early in the 17th century. Samuel Saxon moved from New Kent County, Virginia to Halifax County, North Carolina, and was a planter and well-respected citizen. His son, Benjamine Saxon, Sr., was too old to fight in the Revolutionary War but he had furnished supplies and served with the Colonial Governor to put down insurrection before war was declared. Benjamine married Sarah Green and moved from Halifax County, North Carolina to Burke County, Georgia. They had six children: Joseph, Henry, James (Civil War, killed in Army),

Augusta, Rebecca and Mary. James Saxon was buried at Arlington Cemetery, one of only 300 Confederate soldiers allowed to be buried there.

Henry Saxon (son of Benjamine) became a Methodist Minister and in 1795 married Judith Smith (daughter of Samuel Smith, Revolutionary soldier of Edgecombe County, NC). Benjamine Archelus Saxon was born of this marriage. Judith Saxon died in about 1832 and in 1838 Rev. Henry Saxon married Elizabeth Oliver Hale, a young widow of North Carolina, and after several years in Randolph County, he moved to Florida, where he reared his second family. He is buried about three miles from Tallahassee.

Rev. Henry Saxon's letter to his son, Joseph, is illustrative of the caliber of man he was:

Tallahassee, Florida, July 15, 1853
To Joseph Tarpley Saxon, Oklahoma
My Respected and Dear Sir:

I am much grateful to receive your kind letter of the 16th of March, last, which brought the pleasing intelligence of your prosperity, and the little object of your earthly hopes. May Heaven smile upon you, your wife and little son; and give you both much future happiness in him. Now, my son Joseph, raise your son in the nurture and admonition of the Lord, and train him up in the way he should go, that when he is old he may not depart from it; first give yourselves to the Lord, and by your examples and precepts teach your child the holy religion of the Saviour Jesus, that you may all become the joint heirs with Christ of the everlasting Kingdom of God. Oh how it would rejoice my heart to hear that you were enjoying the sweet comforts of religion and were in the high road to Heaven, so that if we never meet again in this world we might have a prospect of meeting in the Kingdom of Glory. Now let me pray you, as with my dying words, try to meet me in Heaven, for I hope to get to that happy place; disappoint me not.

My crop this year is very sorry. We had no rain sufficient to wet the ground more than half an inch from the 22nd of March until the 2nd of June, so that my corn crop is cut quite short, and my cotton never came up until sometime in June. Now as touching your worldly prospects, they are flattering, but do not let them win your heart from God. May your health be good, therefore prepare for the solemn hour. Benjamin wishes to hear from you, and says that you must write to him, and let him know your P. O. address. All the children are anxious to see you, and send their love to you.

S. D. Kirk is dead; throwed from a horse and killed without uttering a word as any heard. This should be a warning to us all. Your step-mother desires to be remembered, and gives her love to yourself and wife.

You both have my warmest love and parental affections.
Your Father,
Henry Saxon

The previous letter was one of two letters written by Rev. Henry Saxon and preserved in the book, *Martin and Allied Families.* The other letter was written to his nephew Albert B. Saxon of Richmond County, Augusta, GA. Later descendants carried the name Richmond, including Eli Richmond Saxon, the paternal grandfather of Jean, Emmett, Ben and Emily Saxon.

Research revealed that the Saxon family of Tallahassee was related through the marriage of Carolyn Saxon to prominent physician and pioneer settler of Albany, Georgia, Dr. Talliaferro Jones. Dr. Jones was a direct descendant of Captain John Talliaferro of Revolutionary War fame. Another link, through Mary Dunwoody Saxon, was to Mittie Bullock of Bullock Hall, mother of President Theodore Roosevelt.

On June 6, 1913, the Stone Castle Chapter of the D.A.R. (Daughters of the American Revolution) presented a silver loving cup to Alice Glaze Lowrey, organizer and first regent. Alice was a descendant of Reverend Henry Saxon and an enthusiastic patriot in city and state organizations of the D.A.R., Colonial Dames, Daughters of 1812, and Daughters of the Confederacy.

When Ben shared the family findings with Emmett, he was interested, but not excited about his illustrious background. Because Paula and her siblings had different fathers, she was not part of this heritage hunt, but her half-sisters, Jean and Emily were, and they were thrilled to the bone to be informed that they had American pioneer blood running through their veins. It became a point of pride from then on for each of them, especially Emily, who had not even known she was a Saxon until 1985. Several years later, in 1997, Jean and Emily joined the United Daughters of the Confederacy together. Emily is still a member to this day, and while Jean has let her membership lapse, there is no denying that she is of good solid stock and qualifies for any of the ancestral organizations that have sprung up over the past two centuries. Now, thanks to Ben's extensive research, Jean and Emily know that they and their progeny have a right, by blood, to be members of:

> Colonial Dames of America National Society
> Colonial Dames of 17th Century
> Founders & Patriots
> Sons & Daughters of the Pilgrims
> Daughters of the American Revolution
> Daughters of American Colonists
> Daughters of 1812
> Daughters of the Confederacy

> Sons of American Revolution
> Children of the American Revolution
> First Families of Virginia
> Society of Colonial Wars
> World War I Armistice 11-1918
> American Legion

Yes, there was no doubt about it ... Ben was determined that the Saxon name was going to be respected again, and his genealogical research was part of that goal. As a teacher and student of history, Ben enjoyed seeking his own history and found it interesting and compelling. He is a long-time member and past-president of the Sons of the American Revolution in addition to receiving many teaching awards and recognitions from the D.A.R. and S.A.R. over the years.

Reverend Henry Saxon, Ben's ancestor, closed his letter to his son with "warmest love and parental affection." Those were emotions that Ben always wished for in his parents, but never found. Now, through his tenacious research, Ben has received a century-old message of love from a respected ancestor, and he is happy to pass that on to his children, grandchildren and future generations of Saxons.

Chapter Nine

Memorials

This book is dedicated to three men who enriched the Saxon heritage while still in this earthly realm, sharing and passing on the bloodline, in the case of Emmett Saxon, Jr. and Bruce Acree, and fathering descendants, in the case of Harry Acree. Each of these fine men left a legacy that lives in the hearts of the Saxon progeny today.

Emmett Richmond Saxon, Jr., the second of four children born to Emmett Richmond Saxon and Christine Saxon, died on April 19, 2010 at the age of 66 in Nettleton, Mississippi. A man who earned his living and supported his family for more than 40 years as a long-distance truck driver, Emmett was a faithful member of Crosspointe Fellowship Church and was chosen Mason of the Year in 2008 by his brothers at the Nettleton Masonic Lodge #451. A devoted son of God

Saxon Brothers, Ben and Emmett

and loving brother to Jean Saxon Acree, Ben Lee Saxon, Emily Scoggins Mullings, and half-sister Paula Woodall Manning, Emmett was a widower at the time of his death and father of Loressa Saxon, as well as step-father to Elizabeth Shackelford Brown.

Although Emmett lived far from his siblings geographically, he was always in close touch with his older sister, Jean, and through her, with the rest of the family. "Emmett and I talked on the phone nearly every day," recalls Jean. "I would ask him what he was doing and he would talk about the cowboy movie he was watching, or tell me about getting up early that morning to take food to the homeless. He did that nearly every morning, even after he got so ill. He was such a good

Jean, Emmett, Emily & Ben

man, always wanting to give back to those less fortunate. Emmett was loved and respected by the people in his community. The church was completely full on the day of his funeral, and there was even a special plaque made in his honor. Emmett had a hard life, but he had a heart of gold and he shared what he had with others."

Ben's daughter, Meredith, remembers her Uncle Emmett with great love. "Uncle Emmett always had a garden. He was a hard worker who took good care of his family. He enjoyed cooking and taking care of others at home and in the community. He looked forward to us coming to visit him."

Growing up, Emmett and his brother, Ben, were often separated by age at the Mercy Home, but the brothers remained close and spent as much time together as they could. When Emmett aged out of the Mercy Home and was put up for foster care, Ben chose to go with him. They were brothers, after all, and Ben wanted to be with his brother as long as he could. Even after they were separated by the system and other

Emmett & Ben

circumstances, Ben and Emmett stayed in contact as much as possible. Later, when Emmett was living with their big sister, Jean, and helping her care for her infant son, Ben was in touch with them and saw them occasionally. When Jean married Harry, Emmett lived with them for a while and Ben would sometimes come and spend weekends with them. Those were special weekends when Ben and Emmett and Harry enjoyed time together and had time to bond with Bruce, too, with Jean there, loving all of them. Eventually, after he moved temporarily with Harry and Jean and family to West Virginia, Emmett decided to pursue his lifelong career as a truck driver, and moved permanently to Nettleton, Mississippi. "My brother, Emmett, carried the effects of our rough childhood with him all his life, but in spite of everything, he worked hard and became a productive member of society, a responsible family man and was respected in his church and community," says Ben, noting that Emmett suffered from rickets as a result of malnourishment as a very young child and also was affected emotionally and intellectually by mistreatment and neglect. Throughout their young years, Emmett was consistently behind Ben academically and developmentally, probably due to the fact that he was older and had been exposed to harsher treatment before Ben was born, and also because, while Ben was innately defiant and determined, Emmett's nature was more laid back and accepting.

As a teacher with more than forty years of experience, many of them working with youngsters who, like Emmett, were damaged by circumstances beyond their control, Ben is proud of his brother for accomplishing what he did in his too-short life. "Emmett was living proof that you can overcome whatever life hands you and become a good citizen."

Harry Eugene Acree died at the age of 76 on October 18, 2011 in Ocala, Florida. The son of Hazel Hill and Juanita Bolin Acree of West Virginia, Harry was the beloved husband of Jean Saxon Acree, father of daughters Dianna (Sissy) and Stacy, and step-father of Bruce Wayne Acree. Harry had three grand-children, Josh, Katie and Amanda, and one great-granddaughter, Autumn Rose, at the time of his death. He is remembered as a man of God ... a good man who was loved and respected by all who knew him.

A former coal miner, Harry worked for many years as a mechanic and could be relied upon to fix just about anything that was powered by an engine, and always a hard worker, he kept busy even after retirement, working on lawn mowers and doing repairs on other appliances.

"Harry was the best husband anyone could ever want," says Jean. "He was such a nice man. If there was something I wanted to do, I could do it and know he would support me when I did it. We were married 49 years when he passed away and I still catch myself thinking, 'I need to tell Harry about that,' and then realize he's gone. He was the love of my life and I miss him every hour of every day."

Harry wanted a son and Jean has always said he fell in love with Bruce before he fell in love with her. "Bruce was 3 years old when I met Harry and he adopted him as soon as he could," says Jean. "Harry loved Bruce like he was his own son." When his daughter, Stacy, and her husband, Jon, presented Harry with grandson, Josh, he was thrilled. Harry had wanted a grandson to play baseball with and take fishing. Josh adored Harry and the little boy was the apple of his grandfather's eye, but unfortunately, Harry passed away when Josh was still very young.

A compassionate and generous man with a great sense of humor, Harry enjoyed his large family, especially after his wife, Jean, and her brothers, Ben and Emmett, were finally able to add two more sisters and their children to the mix. When any of his nieces or nephews needed him, Harry was there for them.

Harry's nephew, Mike Mullings (Emily's second son) remembers a day when he and Uncle Harry worked for hours doing a brake job on a Honda. "We were both scratching our heads a bit," says Mike, "but he was a 'get her done' kind of guy and he finally helped me get it all back together." Calling his late uncle a "good ole boy – just as nice as you could get," Mike grins. "He had some of the best jokes, too, but I probably can't get into that here."

148

Scott Mullings (Emily's youngest son) remembers watching football with his Uncle Harry whenever he visited him at home. One summer, Scott remembers, they traveled to Alabama with Uncle Harry and others in the family and met up with Uncle Emmett. It was in Alabama that Scott learned to swim and rolled a four-wheeler, and both of his uncles, Harry and Emmett, were there. "Uncle Harry would motivate you to 'Man up' and do what you had to do and not whine about it," recalls Scott, remembering that summer.

Ben's daughter, Meredith Saxon Ritacco, remembers her Uncle Harry as a good person who loved to watch football games on television. She fondly remembers him as a "West Virginia Mountaineer" who was a very hard worker.

Calling his Uncle Harry a "family man and a story teller," Glenn Mullings (Emily's oldest son), cherishes the memories of Harry, including the most vivid ones of Harry in his recliner out in the Florida room watching football. Harry rarely missed a football game on television. He had a Gator hat and some shirts, mainly because his daughters loved the Gators, but Harry did not discriminate – he loved all sports, especially football and baseball, and watched whatever sporting event was on the tube.

Harry's daughters, Sissy and Stacy, knew that they could get away with just about anything with their Dad. He was not the disciplinarian in their family – that job definitely belonged to their mother, Jean. Jean admits that sometimes the girls thought she was a warden when she laid down the rules. Sometimes, though, when one of them would ask Harry for permission to do something, and he said, "Ask your Mother," they would get a reprieve and Jean would tell them to ask their Dad again. So, unless Jean was in "warden-mode," the Acree girls had a pretty easy time getting their way.

Harry liked for his family to sit down together at the dinner table and whenever possible, Jean would make sure dinner waited until he got home from work. If any of the kids got a little rowdy at the dinner table, a quick whistle from Harry was all it took to calm things down. "You could hear a pin drop after Dad whistled," recalls Stacy.

Even when discipline was meted out by Jean, it did not in any way resemble the harsh treatment she and her brothers received as children at the Mercy Home, and Harry always backed her up on whatever method of discipline she chose. For example, when Sissy decided to skip school with a bunch of older high school girls, they were picked up by the police and Jean received a call from school. When Sissy got home, Jean handed her a notebook and a pen and said, "You need to sit down there and write 'I will not skip school' 500 times. Hours later, when she finally finished writing, Jean took the pages from her and tore them to bits. She never forgot that lesson and she never skipped school again. "There was a method in my madness," says Jean with a grin. "It also helped with her handwriting in school!"

Stacy loved school and never skipped. Her teacher was so impressed with Stacy's work that her teacher wanted to help her get a job when she graduated, so she was sent to work at Vining Heating & Air, where she met her ex-husband, Jon Vining. Later, the teacher joked, "I sent you there to get a job ... not a husband!!" Although Stacy and Jon have since divorced, they are the doting parents of Josh, who was the apple of his Grandfather Harry's eye. Josh was about five years old when he sang "Jesus Loves Me" at Harry's funeral and the entire congregation applauded.

Joshua Vining
Baptism Day

Harry's brother, Larry, lives out in Salt Lake City, Utah, and several years ago, Harry, Jean, Sissy and her husband, Thomas, and their daughter, Katie, traveled to Utah to see Larry. They took in the Mormon Tabernacle and were amazed at the salt flats and all the animals that were there, including bison and goats. Jon Vining's family is Mormon and Josh was baptized in October of 2014 in the Mormon faith.

Stacy's former sister-in-law lives in Boulder, Colorado, where her husband is a professor at the University of Colorado. "They live in a glass house - really," marvels Jean. "Meredith, Stacy and I went to visit them and stayed for a couple of weeks. We had a good time. Ben's daughter, Meredith, is my God-daughter. She and Ben's son, Robert, have always been close to Harry and me and our children. Harry and Robert always got along so well – they kidded each other every chance they got."

Bruce Wayne Acree, Jean's beloved son born of her first marriage and adopted at age three by Harry Acree, who fell in love with his mother AFTER he fell in love with Bruce. A cute little blonde boy whose first couple of years were spent with his hard-working mother after she left his father, Bruce had loving care from his Uncle Emmett while Jean worked long hours to put a roof over their heads.

A "cotton-top" like his Uncle Ben, Bruce, also like Ben, always walked to the beat of a different drummer. He was a loving son to his mother and a respectful boy to his step-father, Harry, but he also wanted to know his roots and made a point of visiting his biological father in Texas and independently pursuing his own interests, whether they went along with those of his family or not. Bruce also inherited Ben's intelligence and abiding interest in history. He loved his Saxon heritage. He and his Uncle Ben enjoyed a camaraderie that included much shared laughter over some of the hilarious Hagar the Horrible cartoons about Saxons that Bruce would cut out from the funny papers and present with mock solemnity to his uncle.

HAGAR THE HORRIBLE

"Bruce was interested in history and he was particularly fascinated by his mother's side of the family. He was always asking questions about his Saxon heritage," says Ben, "and, like his ancestors, both Saxon and Indian (on his grandmother, Christine's side), Ben was a free spirit and a wanderer." Calling his nephew an adventurer and an explorer, Ben notes that Bruce explored several careers including working as an automobile mechanic, a nurse's aide in infirmaries and as a highly skilled medical technician.

Shy and quiet as a boy, Bruce was unassuming and helpful. He emulated his step-dad, Harry, in that he would do just about anything anyone asked of him – even to the point of seeing things to be done before anyone asked. For instance, when Jean came home late from work, she would often walk in to the welcoming aroma of a good meal cooked for the family by her son, Bruce.

Once in a great while, Bruce and his sisters, Stacy and Sissy, would be invited to visit their grandmother, Christine, whose husband, Travis, was notoriously unfriendly. If Travis was absent from their grandmother's house, they would spend time with her feeding her goats and working in her garden, but as soon as Travis showed up, they would be out of there. Bruce was the exception. For some reason, Travis took a liking to Bruce ... not exactly affection, but at least tolerance. Jean remembers that once, as a baby, Bruce took his little finger out of his mouth and ran it through the gravy bowl on the table, and Travis actually found it amusing. Travis had made it clear to Christine that he wanted nothing to do with her children or grandchildren. "I didn't raise my kids and I sure as hell am not going to raise yours!" he said in no uncertain terms. So, the fact that he didn't yell at that cute little blonde baby, Bruce, dipping his finger in the gravy is so rare that it is, indeed, memorable.

As a teenager, Bruce traveled to Texas where his biological father lived. He was destined to spend quite a bit of time in Texas over the next few years, but he always returned to his Saxon roots in Ocala. His true "heart" parents were Harry and Jean, and he was glad to see his uncles, aunts and cousins when he came to town.

Because he was so often absent from family events and was also quite a bit older than Ben's and Emily's children, his cousins have few recollections of him, except that he was quiet and loved his family. One family trip that Bruce did take with his Saxon relatives was when they traveled to the funeral of his maternal grandmother, Christine. He was one of the few at that gravesite that had only good memories of his grandmother, whose controlling, violent husband had, for some strange reason, decided that sweet, quiet little blonde boy was an "acceptable Saxon."

Bruce, far right, with family at Grandmother Christine's gravesite

Sadly, Bruce died an untimely death as the result of a pulmonary embolism on September 22, 2013 at the young age of 54. He left behind a daughter, Amanda D., and a granddaughter, Autumn Rose. He also left behind another arrow in the already broken heart of his mother, Jean, who, in the course of just three years – from 2010 to 2013 – lost her dear brother, Emmett, her beloved husband, Harry, and her only son, Bruce.

"It is more than one person can bear," says Jean. The sun, somehow, continues to rise in the morning and set in the evening, but life will never be the same for those who remain behind. Jean spends more time alone these days, reading and thinking and remembering. "I thank God that I still have my brother, Ben," she says. "He is the only one left who really knows about the hard life we've lived."

Now, as she focuses her love on her daughters, grandchildren, and siblings, Jean Saxon Acree continues to exhibit that same strong pioneer spirit that was so evident as she and her brothers came to age at the Mercy Home, each of them determined to "do something and be somebody," regardless of the low expectations others had of them.

Chapter Ten

The Next Generation

When Ben's children, Meredith and Robert, won grand prizes with their Science Fair Exhibits and were written up in the newspaper, it was tangible evidence that the next generation of Saxons was on the way to making up for the humiliating childhood of their father and two of his siblings. Unlike his mother, Ben cared greatly that his children got to school and he also cared what they did when they got there.

Ben was protective of his daughter, Meredith, a pretty, well-behaved child who caused few, if any, problems growing up. It was difficult for him to show affection because he had grown up with so little feminine attention or affection, but neither of his

6B Ocala Star-Banner   Sunday, March 7, 1982

TWO OF GRACE CHURCH DAY SCHOOL SCIENCE FAIR GRAND AWARD WINNERS
. . . Meredith Saxon, won grand prize, fourth grade; and her brother, Robert, grand prize, second grade

Grace School Announces Grade Winners For Science Exhibits

Grace Episcopal School officials have announced the winners from all eight grades in the school's science fair.

Students were judged on creative ability, scientific thought, thoroughness, skill and clarity. A perfect score was a 100, with the first two criteria earning the most potential points. Judges were Frank Holland, Jim Wetz and Al Wilson.

Winners from grade one were Brooke Short, first place; Stacy Berman, second; Krista Tucker and Beth Newnam, third; and Dawn Lance, Brooke Weiner, Robert Noell, Katherine Smith and Jenny Polwort, honorable mention.

Grade two winners were Robert Saxon, grand prize; Heather Staples, first place; Teddy Schatt, second place; Melissa Roberts, Amy Murphy and Bryan Deck, third place; and Amy Cundiff, Piper Fleming, Terri Manche, JoElla Barrett, Matt Daubenmire, Teresa Lewis, Chad Sutton, Donnie Boeff, Amy Bachman, Jeremy Hudson, Mike Bruns, Tom Christmas and Larry Mills, honorable mention.

Third grade winners were Jana Hope, grand prize; Lili Kennelly, first place; Jude Gasparro, second place; Bill Moeller, third place; and Tag Townsend, honorable mention.

Fourth grade winners were Meredith Saxon, grand prize; Pat McLaughlin and Katy Hagan, first place;

Bobby Morrow and Jennifer Chalkley, second place; and Christian Amatea and Chip Williams, third place.

Fifth grade winners were Todd Behrends, grand prize; Heidi Hester and Lisa Sieger, first place; Scott Ritter, second place; Meredith Silver and Melissa Nix, third place; and Chip Conley, John Steinberg and Gina Hutcheson, honorable mention.

Sixth graders winners were Lori Duvoll, grand prize; Ken Crooks, first place; Warren Taylor, second place; Jessica Otto, third place; and Sue Griffith, Jocelyn Massaro, Danny MacCartney and Dee Fitzgerald.

Seventh grade winners were Tiffany Baker, grand prize; Dennis Gallagher, first place; Buff Moring, second place; Franci Hanley, third place; and Caren Colburn, Michele Duncan, Frank Behrends and Kana Roess, honorable mention.

Eighth grade winners were Lynn Moeller, grand prize; Dawn Kennelly, first place; Jill Hester, second place; Victoria Mathis, third place; and Cara Pagano, Valeria Williams, Julie Harris, Jeanelle Jackson and Michelle Jenkins, honorable mention.

Also taking first places were the class projects by the first grade and kindergarten 4-year-olds and 5-year-olds.

kids had any doubt that they were loved by their father. "You grow up like I did and you don't know what love is," says Ben. "It's almost like you skipped that phase in growing up, and yet, when you have children, you learn to love from the

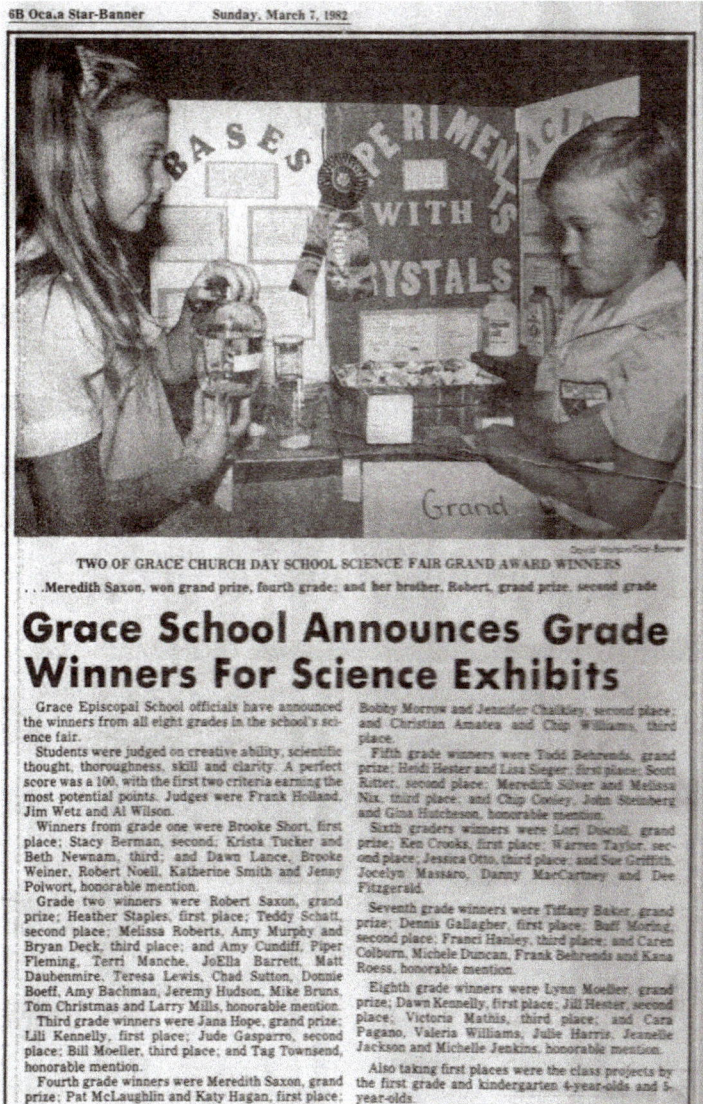

first day forward, being attentive to every whim." Today, Ben truly enjoys being a loving grandfather to his five grandchildren.

Robert was a handful from the beginning. "Too much like his daddy," jokes Ben, grinning. Robert used to complain that he couldn't do a thing in the town of Ocala without Ben hearing about it, and that was true. Ben's students and the other teachers kept him informed. "I once got a call that Robert had been bull-riding and, for a while, I just went ahead and let him do it," says Ben. "One day he came in and told me about it. He said, 'I hurt my back. I can't do it anymore."

Putting his children in private school was a decision that Ben made because he felt they would be forced to reach their full potential. Robert was not his teacher's favorite student in public school, as he was acting up and his teacher insisted he be tested for ADD or some other disorder. It turned out, after placing him in private school, that Robert had not been behaving "because he was bored to tears," according to his Dad. Ben started teaching him to read at home and by the time he was in second grade, he knew most of the answers. One of the teachers told Ben that his son was like he used to be – he didn't answer questions in class but if he was asked he knew the answer. "He gets it by osmosis."

Ben is exceptionally proud of his children. "They both had the strength to choose a career and go for it," he says. "I have always said I didn't care what field they went into as long as they did their best at it, no halfway stuff. So far they are both doing just that."

Today, Robert is 6'3' and solid as a rock. He has made his father extremely proud. Robert Saxon holds a leadership position as Commercial Sales Manager at Certified Slings & Supply in the Orlando, Florida area, with responsibility for six Central Florida Counties. A graduate of the Booth School of Business in Chicago, Robert married Michelle Lynn Batlemente on February 29th, 2008, and Ben was the best man at his wedding. At the time of this writing, Robert and Michelle are the parents of Mason Lee Saxon, 5, and Lauren Grace Saxon, 3.

Mason Lee and Lauren Grace Saxon

Meredith, now a Speech Pathologist for the Highlands County School System in Lake Placid, also has her own private practice named Sundance Studios, and works often with students from the Florida School for the Deaf and Blind. She and her husband, Mike Ritacco, have three children: Isabelle, 7, Michael, 5, and Ava, 3. When asked about what her Dad, the teacher, taught her, Meredith responded:

If there is anything my ... family has taught me is that there is NOTHING more important than family. No amount of money in the world could make that better. Blood is blood, no matter where you have been or where you are going. I was taught that perseverance gets you everywhere. Make a life for yourself and be strong in it. Because one day, family will go on to the heavens and in your mind you need to know that you can and will move on. Strength in our family can be a curse, but it gets us our will to survive and learn to be with each other. We all may not see each other every day, talk every day or get together at family holidays or functions, but as a fact, we do know that if we were all put in a room tomorrow, we would just act like we saw each other yesterday and pick up conversation where we left off. We are close and probably care too much for each other (if possible) ... but we know that no matter what, someone is always there! It doesn't matter where you have been, but where you are headed. If you have strength and family, my Dad has always told me, you can't go wrong. I wouldn't trade anything for my life or upbringing. I can only hope I can instill in my children the same faith my Dad had in us.

A Gift to Ben From Meredith

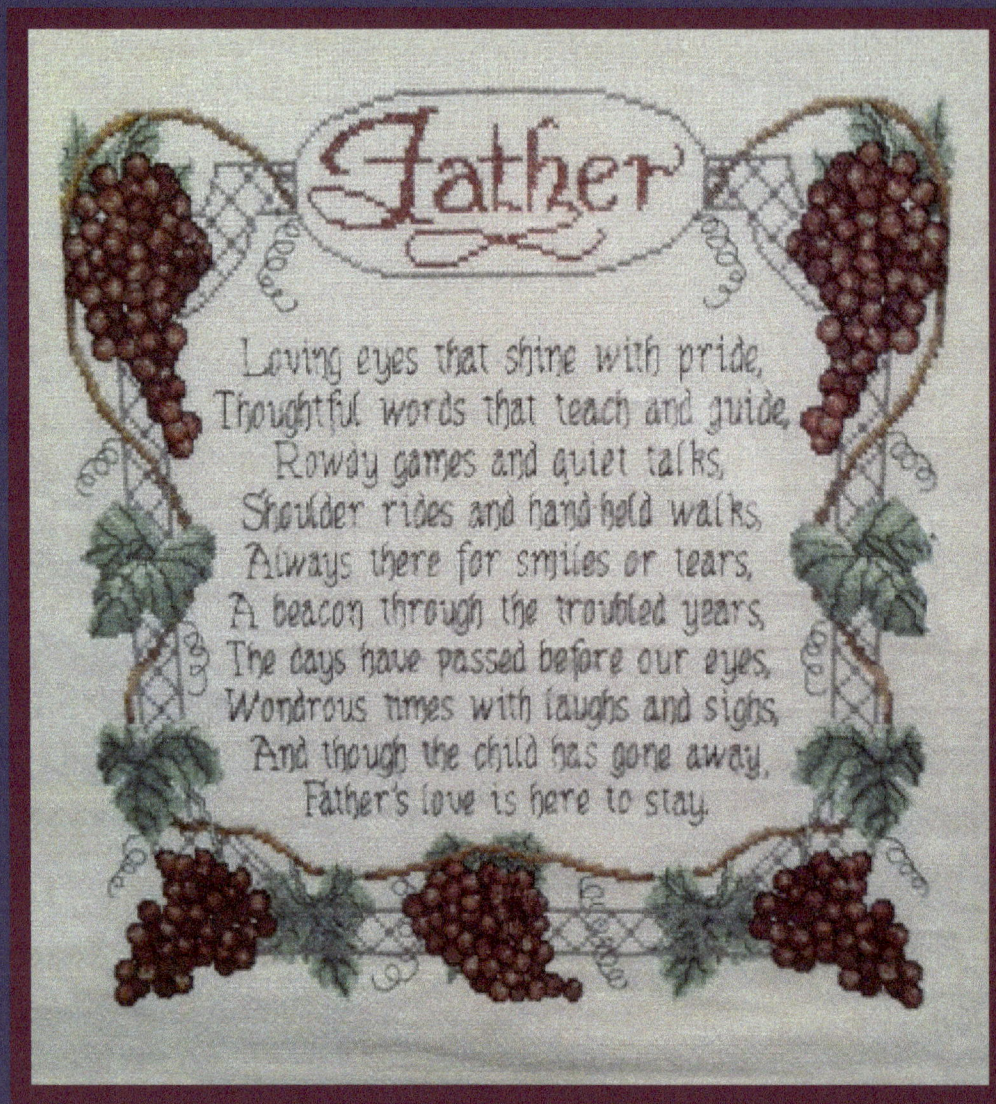

Father

Loving eyes that shine with pride,
Thoughtful words that teach and guide,
Rowdy games and quiet talks,
Shoulder rides and hand-held walks,
Always there for smiles or tears,
A beacon through the troubled years,
The days have passed before our eyes,
Wondrous times with laughs and sighs,
And though the child has gone away,
Father's love is here to stay.

Having been an "empty nester" for some time now, Ben is never completely alone, as he has his "girls" ... Sierra and DJ ... two beautiful German Shepherds.

**Ben's Girls
Sierra and D.J.**

Never having learned the meaning of the word "retirement," he continues to teach virtual classes on-line to more than 40 students per semester, still earning many of the same accolades from his on-line students as he once did in the classroom. One student who had never experienced home schooling before, told Ben, "Mr. Saxon, I learned so much from you, but other than that, I love your class best. I think you are an amazing teacher."

An amazing teacher he is and has been for 46 years. He's taught middle school, high school, junior college, and now virtual school on-line. He's a long-time member of the Florida State Council for Social Studies – responsible for District 6 which encompasses three of the 67 counties in the State – Marion, Alachua and Levy Counties. Voted Teacher of the Year several times and recipient of countless awards from Junior Achievement, the Sons of the American Revolution, Daughters of the American Revolution, and other educational and civic organizations, he has been asked repeatedly to take on leadership positions in the State and County Councils, but has always preferred the one-on-one interaction between student and teacher. Never one to seek glory, Ben is simply satisfied to know that he has made a positive difference in the lives of many students over the years.

The rapport he establishes with his students is unusual. They regard him so highly that they go out of their way at the end of the year to give him gifts, write letters, cards, and pay tribute to him, remembering great teaching moments in his classroom. "My kids would say 'Hey! It's the last day of school! Dad's going to bring us home good stuff!'" recalls Ben, remembering coming home loaded with boxes of Whitman's Samplers and other sweets that he doesn't eat, but wouldn't turn down. Today, gifts, plaques, letters, and photos fill Ben's home office, china cabinets, shelves, desks, walls and bookcases.

Certain "Saxon traditions" became familiar to students year after year. One of the most recognized traditions was Mr. Saxon's famous "Hairy Eyeball." This would occur when Ben raised one eyebrow real high and stared at the student being "eyeballed." It was not necessarily a bad thing ... in fact, the object of the "Hairy Eyeball" usually got a chuckle from the class. While the students considered Ben one of their best teachers because of his mastery of history and the facts they learned, there was also the added bonus of having fun. "Fun was not something I ever had in school, and laughter didn't happen often in my young life," recalls Ben. "I was the poor kid, the foster kid, the Mercy Home kid ... the one that wasn't going to amount to anything no matter what I did. As a teacher, I tried every day to make sure that each student felt worthy and that we got a chance to laugh together. Laughter – especially when it's shared – is a powerful healing tool."

Ben recalls that there were always a few that didn't pass, but by the end of the year, most of his students sensed that he understood them and cared about them. Several years ago, after he started teaching virtual school on-line, a mother called him to thank him for teaching her son and make sure he would be teaching next year for her younger son. She wanted to be sure he would be there when her sons graduated. "She'd never even met me!" says Ben. "I obviously made an impression on her sons and that means a great deal to me ... no hairy eyeball on-line, but I'm still establishing a relationship with my students – teaching them about the subject and about the importance of mutual respect between human beings."

His advice to students: Write your goals. Never let adversity stand in your way ... then you've got it made. I don't care what you do – that's your business – but be the best you can be at it and don't let anybody stop you. You are important.

What God has planned for me is to be the best person I can be at whatever I choose to do. **Be the best you can be at whatever you do.** When you get to be a teenager, tape it to the mirror so you can see it every day.

From early childhood on, the innate Saxon determination of Ben, Jean and Emmett would brook no interference. Their goals – the ones they shared as they were growing up and that Ben, Jean and Emily share today:

1. Improve the name Saxon in the community.
2. Keep family close.
3. Become someone people can look up to as a contributing member of society, not be a problem or loss to society as was expected of us.
4. Get educated and rise above having to do manual labor for a lifetime.
5. Work with others to help them set and achieve goals.
6. Leave a fine legacy for future generations.

"I think each of us has achieved worthwhile goals in our own realms. We have never been a burden on society and we have all been assets in helping others."

In reference to his boyhood ambition to become a veterinarian, Ben notes that he has never truly given up on the idea. Perhaps that is why he has worked so hard training his dogs for all kinds of activities. Financially, it was never possible for him to pursue that career and now, in his late 60's, it would not be feasible to return to college for a veterinary degree. "I think God had other plans for me," he says fatalistically, adding that he has a friend who is a veterinarian at the University of Florida Veterinary School and he has worked with him on various treatments for his dogs as well as shadowing him when he was in practice in New Port Richey. Nevertheless, he knows that his destiny has been to reach the hearts and minds of young people who need someone to believe in them.

As the "Patriarch of the Saxons," Ben has done everything in his power to strengthen the bonds of his family, particularly doing all he can to help his sisters, Jean and Emily, remember the past, stay well in the present, and look forward to the future. As in all families, some are long-distance members and this is the case with Paula Woodall Manning, the daughter of Christine Saxon and half-sister of Jean, Ben, Emmett and Emily. Though she is miles apart from them, Paula thinks often of her siblings, reflecting with love on their commonalities. For instance, Emily gave Paula a rocking chair from her childhood that she treasures. It is almost identical to one Paula had as a child. When she looks at a photo of herself as a girl with a perm and dark-rimmed glasses, she is reminded of her big sister, Jean.

"I looked just like Jean, and now, as we age, Emily and I look more and more alike," says Paula, "and looking like my sisters makes me feel good." Paula regrets that she doesn't get down to Ocala more regularly. She has made plans repeatedly to visit her siblings and something has always interfered – a band concert for a grand-child, a new work schedule, a great-grandbaby's birthday, etc., etc. Although she keeps in touch with Jean and Emily with occasional phone calls and on Facebook, Paula admits that Emmett was the sibling she felt closest to, and she misses him so much. "For some reason, all of this looking for lost sisters affected Emmett more than he let on – he told me that, and even Jean told me that he carried it harder than we knew," Paula says. "Emmett and I were very close. I'd drive up by myself to see him and spend the night there. For some reason, we had a bond of love that was deep. When I talk about my brothers to someone else – I'm proud of both Emmett and Ben. Emmett was a good man who died too young and Ben is an intelligent scholar who has accomplished so much. Jean and Emily both put them-selves through school and taught at college, too, and Emily's a hoot! Jean and Ben are more conservative and Emily's more of a free spirit – I'm proud of all of them."

Something that makes Paula feel more like kin than anything else is when Jean looks at her and tells her she looks and acts just like Christine. "Jean says I'm even built like her," says Paula. "Even though she gave me up – or they took me from her – whatever it was – it was for the best and she was my mother. I know that now. Blood is thicker than water." One strange memory is that Paula was told by her adoptive parents that her foster parents called her "Rickey," which was the name Christine gave to Emily, but maybe she called them both by that name, too. Rickey, Debbie ... whatever she and Emily were called by their biological mother, they were the lucky ones to have been adopted into families that loved them.

Paula's adoptive mother was one of ten children and when she was little, there were 26 grandchildren. On Thanksgiving of 2014, Paula attended a family gathering of more than 75 people and all of them were kin to her, so she and her children and grandchildren are surrounded by loving family in Tuskegee, Alabama. Despite this large, loving family, Paula has enough of her brother Ben in her that she is determined to seek her biological father now that she knows who her biolog-ical mother is. "I got the picture of Mr. Greene and my mother from Ben, and that's all I know about my father ... that his name was Greene and there is this picture of the two of them. I've put it on Facebook and asked if anybody knows these people, even though I'm a person who doesn't want to hurt anybody and, supposedly, the adoption papers say that he was married and had other children. That would mean

I have other siblings and maybe he didn't even know about me. It would be important to me to know if I have other brothers and sisters out there." Paula says her kids are alright with her searching and the girls brought up the medical history, which, until Ben found her, she didn't have a clue about on either side of her parentage. Now, at least, she knows half of it, and then there is that extra sensory perception thing that she shares with her sisters ... once again, Paula mentions a premonition that she feels was significant to her, as the child identified only as "Baby Saxon" finding her four siblings as well as to her present search for her biological father.

"It's ironic," she says. "My husband was jealous and controlling. I took the kids to school every morning and stopped at a little convenience store to get a coke, just to be by myself sometimes. One morning I turned to the news rack at that little store and right in front was some kind of a free little ten page gazette type paper all about lost and found people – ads looking for people – I got a copy of that gazette and came home and poured over it. I put it in a drawer and hid it from my husband because for some reason I didn't want him to know I was looking at that magazine. About a month later, I got the call from Ben. I sensed something was coming. My husband and I have been divorced 24 years now, so I've known about my brothers and sisters even longer than that. Angels come in all different forms. You never know when God is telling you something." Paula was there when her brother, Emmett, passed away, and to this day she treasures the last moments she spent with him in this earthly realm.

Another commonality about the siblings: Emily, a massage therapist, Ben and Jean, teachers, and Paula, a nurse, are all hands-on angels who provide help for hurting people. "Paula has done well with her life," says Emily. "Ben, Jean and I hoped we'd see more of her when we began compiling our family history, and we still do even though we understand that she's a busy registered nurse, a mother, grandmother and now a great-grandmother! Paula cares about helping and healing, just as we all do, and she's even got the extra sensory perception that our mother had. People say we look alike, and I think we do, too. I'm proud to say Paula is our sister."

For Emily, being part of the process of putting together a family memoir has been exciting and inspiring. "I've learned a lot about my past – for instance, I learned that my birth certificate has me listed as a boy – I guess because of the name Clyde Dean – being named after my father's sister, Clyde." Emily has also learned some things about Ben and Jean and Emmett and the rest of the family that she never knew. "And I've realized even more than ever before how lucky I was to be adopted at an early age by good people who truly cared about me. My three older siblings didn't have it easy growing up, like I did, but somehow they made good lives for themselves and raised successful families and became upstanding citizens. They are living proof that God lives inside each of us and if we listen to Him and use the gifts He's given us to the best of our abilities, we will succeed."

Emily still pinches herself once in a while when she thinks of how her life has evolved since she was found by her siblings. "My adopted mother, Cecile, was such a real part of our getting together," says Emily. "She had a strong desire to help me find my family." Not long after Emily reunited with Ben and Jean and Emmett, her adopted mother came down to Ocala to meet them. She highly approved and was happy to meet them. A few years later, she passed away in Gadsden, Alabama and Emily is convinced that she must have known her health wasn't good and wanted to see her daughter reunited with her biological family while she was still alive. "I wish my Daddy had lived to meet my brothers and sisters and their families," says Emily. "He would have loved them all, too. I am blessed. God gave me two families that loved me, and I love them back.

"I wish my parents had lived to see their grown-up grandsons, too. Glenn, our oldest, rose through the ranks working at Winn-Dixie since high school and is now Assistant Store Manager. The fact that he's held a steady job for so long and received regular promotions is an indication of his good character. Determination runs in our family. Michael, our middle son, is so smart. He knows computers inside and out and has worked for a computer company that designs and produces computer animation for professional media companies around the world. Like his older brothers, our youngest son Scott is also a hard worker and a productive citizen. He can do just about anything with his hands and has worked with various aluminum companies fabricating and installing pool enclosures and screened-in porches all over town. Our three sons have given Roger and me four beautiful, healthy grandchildren, Brandon Matthew, Jessica Lee, Sara Elizabeth and Rebecca Madison. We are so proud of our family – past, present and future!"

Far from being loved and cared for by two families, or even by one, Jean was responsible for taking care of her younger siblings from the time she could walk. After her father deserted them, Jean's mother, Christine, gave little Emily up for adoption and put even more responsibility on Jean to take care of the boys. Eventually, seeing that his grandchildren were hungry and neglected, Christine's father, Pop, took them to an orphanage called the Mercy Home. There, they received the bare necessities of life, but no mercy and no love. Jean spent most of her childhood aching for the love of her one remaining parent – her mother, Christine – but it wasn't to be. Christine married a mean, domineering, emotionally abusive man who had no use for her children – so Jean and her brothers grew to adulthood without the love of family, and yet, each of them created their own families. Jean married Harry Acree, a good man, and they raised three good children, Sissy, Stacy and Bruce. Ben and his former wife, Kathy, raised two good children, Meredith and Robert. Emmett and his wife, Helen, raised her daughter Elizabeth and their daughter, Loressa. Paula, surrounded by loving family, raised her four children, Petrina, Pollyanna, Rex and Dennis Ledbetter, to be fine productive citizens. All of their families had roofs over their heads, clothes on their back and food on the table – and most of all, love. But even with love, life and death happens, and within less than three years – between 2010 and 2013 – Jean suffered the tragic loss of her brother Emmett, her husband Harry and her son Bruce. Jean is still reeling from those horrible losses and, for the first time in her life, putting off thinking about what happens next. She spends her days reading voraciously, as she has always done, but now there is a tinge of sadness in her eyes and voice as she rouses herself to go about the daily business of living. Now, more than ever before, she needs the love and concern of family around her.

Jean's daughters, Sissy and Stacy, are in daily contact with their mother and include her regularly in many of their family activities. Jean is proud that both of her daughters have chosen careers in the medical field (Sissy an EMT – Emergency Medical Technician – and Stacy a Paramedic). Her late son, Bruce, was also a medical technician. The fact that her children all chose to provide service that helps to heal people is gratifying to Jean, especially in light of her own emotional pain now and the pain of hunger and deprivation she experienced throughout her childhood. When she thinks of the neglect she experienced as a child, and the heavy responsibility that was placed on her, she is especially thankful for daughters who do thoughtful things like come by to clean her house when she was recently in the hospital. "They must really love me," she says quietly.

Stacy, Paramedic and Sissy, EMT

Just about the only time lately that Jean's smile reaches all the way to her eyes is when mention is made of her 9 year-old grandson, Joshua. "That little stinker!" she declares with a grin. "Joshua will be 10 years old on December 4th ... the day before his Great-Uncle Ben's birthday!" She talks of him asking his mother if she had ever read the book of Joshua in the Bible. "Stacy doesn't have much time to read," says Jean, "but I've read the book of Joshua from front to back and back to front, and one day I'll ask him if he wants to read it with me." She's tried to get Joshua to be a reader, but he's an active little boy who loves to play, so she goes to watch him play baseball and sports right now, and holds in her heart the wish that they will someday read books together.

Jean's oldest grandchild is Sissy's daughter, 28-year old Katie Steppen. Again, Jean smiles brightly when she talks of Katie. "Joshua adores Katie ... says he plans to marry her someday ... and both Katie and Joshua call me G-Mom," she says, adding that she got the idea of G-Mom from her foster-sister, Mary Snider (Aunt Bessie's daughter), whose grandchildren called her by that name. "Katie is a sweetheart," Jean says. "She works at Ocala Eye Clinic, she's got a nice boyfriend, and I've never heard her talk back. If something needs doing, she'll do it. She's a very clean young lady and a good solid person. Her middle name is the same as mine – Jean – and she's my Goddaughter. In fact, several girls in the family are named after me – Ben's daughter Meredith, Emmett's daughter, Loressa, and now, Meredith's daughter, Ava, have my name. Meredith and Ava are also my Goddaughters. I guess they must like me a little bit, for some reason."

Modest about the impact she's had on the lives of the Saxon progeny, including her own children, Jean says that she hopes she's been a good example to them. "No matter what people said to me, I always knew I'd make something of myself and I have," she says. "I married a good man, raised three good kids, worked hard at jobs that helped people, and have been an upstanding citizen all my life. That's what I want for my grandchildren. Whatever they do, I want them to be confident and proud of themselves and know they can do anything they set their mind to." Jean jokes that she's threatened to come back and haunt them if they ever get lazy or try to live off the government. "I'm proud of my kids and grandkids," she says. "They have known all their lives that they are loved. I guess that's the key. Ben and Emmett and I didn't have that in our lives, but we did have Pop (our grandfather who cared enough to take us to the Mercy Home), we did have each other, and we got some religious training along the way, too. We knew about God and, believe it or not, we learned something about love in church. We learned our manners and we knew right from wrong. We did what it took to live right. We got jobs, held them down, built our families, helped them survive, and made good lives. With God's help, we made it happen."

Generations

Parents:

Emmett Richmond Saxon Sr., b. April 8, 1906 – d. March 17, 1971
Christine Fleming Saxon, b. May 2, 1922 – d. Nov. 15, 1980

Children:

• **Jeannette (Jean) Saxon Acree**, b. July 23, 1941
  m. Harry Eugene Acree
  Son: **Bruce Wayne Acree**, b. May 25, 1959 (deceased)
              m. Patricia Rich
                  Daughter: Amanda Dee Acree, b. May 26, 1981
                  Daughter: Autumn Rose, b. Mar. 20, 2008
  Daughter: **Dianna Lynn Acree** (Sissy), b. Sept. 14, 1962
              m. Thomas Peter Steppen
                  Daughter: Katie Jean Steppen, b. June 30, 1986
  Daughter: **Stacy Lee Acree**, b. June 2, 1966
              m/d. Jon Randal Vining
                  Son: Joshua Randal Vining, b. Dec. 4, 2004

• **Emmett Richmond Saxon, Jr.**, b. Aug. 4, 1943 (deceased)
  m. Helen Hendrix
  Daughter: **Loressa Jeannette**, b. July 29, 1969

• **Ben Lee Saxon**, b. Dec. 5, 1945
  m/d. Kathy Elaine Perkins
  Daughter: **Meredith Jeannette**, b. Jan. 24, 1972
              m. Michael Robert Ritacco Sr. b. Sept 5, 1968
                  Daughter: **Isabelle Christine**, b. Dec. 28, 2007
                  Son: **Michael Robert, Jr.**, b. Aug. 3, 2009
                  Daughter: **Ava Jean**, b. Jan. 24, 2011
  Son: **Robert Tremaine**, b. Dec. 21, 1974
              m. Michelle Lynn Batlemente, b. Sept. 20, 1975
                  Son: **Mason Lee**, b. Jan. 30, 2009
                  Daughter: **Lauren Grace**, b. June 14, 2011

• **Clyde Dean (Emily-Emmaline) Saxon Scoggins**, b. Aug. 26, 1947
  (Adopted May 7th, 1953 by Virgil and Cecile Scoggins)
  m. Roger A. Mullings
  Son: **Glenn Allen Mullings**, b. Sept. 11, 1968
              m/d. Terri Ann Mullings, Oct. 23, 1968
                  Son: **Brandon Matthew**, b. Mar. 21, 1991

Daughter: **Jessica Lee,** b. May 25, 1993
Son: **Michael David Mullings**, b. Aug. 17, 1971
Shannon Wagner
Daughter: **Rebecca Madison**, b. July 24, 2003
Son: **Scott Patrick Mullings**, b. Jan. 5, 1977
m/d. Alaishia Mullings
Daughter: **Sara Elizabeth Mullings**, b. July 22, 1999

• **Paula Woodall Manning**, b. Aug. 29, 1951
(Adopted Feb. 13, 1952 by Frances L. Story Woodall and Paul Hollis Woodall)
m/d. Donald Rex Ledbetter, Sr., Larry Manning
Son: **Donald Rex Ledbetter, Jr.,** b. July 11, 1969
m/d. Philesia Borland / Tamara Kever (mother of Tres)
Son: **Donald Rex Ledbetter III** (Tres), b. Nov. 7, 2001
Son: **Dennis Paul Ledbetter**, b. June 17, 1970
m/d. Denise Sullivan (Josh's mom)/Michelle Harper (Paige's mom)/Pam White
Son: **Joshua Paul Ledbetter**, b. Aug. 11, 1987
m. Ashley Chappell
Daughter: **Alyssa Raleigh**, b. Dec. 18, 2013
Step-Dtr.: **Alexis Kaleigh**, b. Dec. 31, 2006
Daughter: **Emily Paige Ledbetter**, b. Sept. 8, 1992

Daughter: **Pollyanna Frances Ledbetter Fitzgerald**, b. Mar. 30, 1975
Tracy Spivey (father of Korey deceased)/m/d. Russell Barker/John Fitzgerald
Son: **Austin Korey Lane Spivey**, b. Sept. 5, 1992
Son: **Ayden Gunner Spivey**, b. Mar. 4, 2014
(Ayden's mother: Brittany McRae)
Daughter: **Alexa Brianna Barker**, b. Sept 19, 1995
Son: **Braden Russell Blaine Barker**, b. Jan. 4, 1997
Son: **John Cade Fitzgerald**, b. Oct. 14, 2001

Daughter: **Petrina Dawn Ledbetter Hornsby**, b. Mar. 23, 1980
m/d. Matthew Cobb/m. Leonard Chris Hornsby
Daughter: **Alena Henley Cobb**, b. Sept. 5, 1999
Son: **Leonard Payton Hornsby**, b. Nov. 14, 2001

Susan D. Brandenburg

Award-winning biographer Susan D. Brandenburg lives in Jacksonville, Florida, and has the great privilege of writing full-length biographies about fascinating people like the Saxon siblings. A seasoned journalist, genealogist, speaker and researcher, she has written weekly columns and feature articles for newspapers, as well as articles for local, state and national magazines. As president of Susan the Scribe, Inc., Susan is a pioneer in the field of writing and publishing. Currently working on her 21st manuscript, Susan thanks God daily for the words that allow her to preserve the amazing legacies of His children.

www.ingramcontent.com/pod-product-compliance
Lightning Source LLC
Chambersburg PA
CBHW041603260326
41914CB00011B/1374